An Angel a Day

• A BOOK OF MEDITATIONS •

An Angel a Day

Stories of
Angelic Encounters

ANN SPANGLER

ZondervanPublishingHouse
Grand Rapids, Michigan

A Division of HarperCollins*Publishers*

Requests for information should be addressed to:
    Zondervan Publishing House
    Grand Rapids, Michigan   49530

Library of Congress Cataloging-in-Publication Data

Spangler, Ann.
    An angel a day / Ann Spangler.
        p. cm.
    ISBN: 0-310-48720-X
    1. Angels—Biblical teaching—Meditations. I. Title.
BT966.2.S63   1994
235'.3—dc20   94-28206
                                                         CIP

Cover design by David Marty
Cover photo: SUPERSTOCK/Angel, Bernardino Luini
Interior design by Sherri L. Hoffman

Printed in the United States of America

94 95 96 97 98 99 00 01 02 03 /❖ DC / 10 9 8 7 6 5 4 3 2 1

This edition is printed on acid-free paper and meets the American National Standards Institute Z39.48 standard.

For My Parents
With Gratitude and Affection

CONTENTS

$\mathcal{N}$OTE TO THE READER ↝

A number of the Scripture passages quoted in the text refer to "the angel of the Lord." Some biblical scholars believe that this phrase, particularly in the earlier books of the Old Testament, refers to God himself. Others believe that it refers to an actual angel, who closely represents the Almighty. Many of the early church fathers tended to recognize the preincarnate Christ in these passages. Whatever the case, readers can fruitfully reflect on these passages, knowing that angels reflect the glory of God and are active in our world only to do his bidding.

Special thanks is due to the many people who so gladly shared their stories with me. In each case, their willingness to speak of such things seemed to spring from a desire for others to experience the kindness of God as they have. I owe a special debt of gratitude to Mark Kinzer for reading the text for theological accuracy. Of course, any errors in the text are solely the responsibility of the author.

*I*NTRODUCTION ॐ

Why Talk about Angels?

When I was a less-than-cherubic child of four or five, I entertained a variety of unorthodox notions about the universe and my place in it. Knowing nothing of the Bible at that time, my child's mind tried to make sense out of some of the deeper questions of life. Chief among these was the question of where I had come from. I could not quite believe that a person of my intelligence and importance had not even existed before that blustery day in March of 1950 when I entered the scene.

My parents did their best to teach me my prayers, take me to church, and explain that God deserved the credit for making me. Still, I wondered if God hadn't created me somewhere in the clouds (where I thought heaven was) and only later sent me down to join my family on earth. No doubt I had been influenced by paintings I had seen of chubby little angels bouncing from cloud to cloud, their wings firmly glued to shoulders about the size of mine. More than anything, I wanted to believe that I too had once had wings and would someday have them again. Though I did not understand my desires then, I believe now that I longed for the freedom that the angels possessed and for the ability to move at will between heaven and earth. Somehow, I felt too heavy for my years, unfairly chained by gravity to the natural world when I so desired to soar into the skies where I imagined God to be. So strong was my desire to be airborne that, like many children who grew up watching Clark Kent transform himself into Superman, I even attempted a disastrous flight down the living room stairs.

Such experiences were to alter my views drastically. But they did not change my desire for a deeper connection with God and with the unseen world he had created. Years later I have come to understand his mercy and his plan of salvation, accomplished through the life and death of Jesus of Nazareth. I have also come to cherish and to believe the Bible, which tells the unfolding story of God's love for us and his plan for the human race.

Page after page of the Scriptures describe the long struggle between God and the men and women he created to know him. It is a story of mercy, miracles, rebellion, treachery, wrath, repentance, nick-of-time rescues, and ultimate salvation. The cast of characters includes not only the Creator himself and the countless men and women he has made but angels, both good and evil.

Too often, though, we ignore the role that angels play. Many Christians are afraid that talk of angels will distract from the power and majesty of God. And many others have a hard time taking angels at all seriously. But as John Calvin has said, "The angels are the dispensers and administrators of the Divine beneficence toward us; they regard our safety, undertake our defense, direct our ways and exercise a constant solicitude that no evil befall us."

Like it or not, angels are important players in the drama of salvation. Isn't it time we paid a little more attention to these powerful and loving allies that God has given us? True, there are dangers. We must never forget that worship belongs only to God, no matter how beautiful or powerful some of his creatures may be. We must also remember that angels are but one way that God works in the universe. Pascal said, "We create angels, but trouble comes if we create too many." They aren't the whole story, nor even the most important part of the story. They are simply supporting actors, servants of the living God, as we are. Even so, such fears fail to justify our ignorance of the angels. Knowing more about their nature and purpose will help us to perceive more of God's own majesty and his loving plan for our lives.

I have delved into the pages of the Bible and listened to the stories of people of faith in the hopes of both satisfying my own curiosity and offering comfort and encouragement to anyone who longs for a deeper connection with God. The skepticism and rationalism of our age have not smothered our desire for the spiritual dimension of life. If anything, such attitudes have merely created a pent-up thirst that only God can quench.

I hope that these reflections will increase your thirst and your desire to know God as you become aware of the heavenly allies he has given you. If we let them, angels can be a window to God, offering a glimpse of his power, his goodness, and his loving intentions toward us. It's time to put aside a materialistic view of the universe in favor of a thoroughly biblical one. With this book, I hope to do in writing what a painter by the name of Sir Edward Coley Burne-Jones accomplished in his art: "The more materialistic science becomes, the more angels shall I paint: their wings are my protest in favor of the immortality of the soul."

One

The Gift of Angels

*Every good and perfect gift is from above, coming
down from the Father of the heavenly lights.*
—JAMES 1:17

*H*ow would you feel if you gave someone a gift that they refused to open? Wouldn't you be disappointed and a bit hurt? I sometimes wonder if that's how God feels about the angels, wonderful gifts he has given to protect, inspire, and lead us safely home to him. Yet we neglect the angels through our indifference, ignorance, and incorrigible skepticism.

The angels are part of God's ingenious provision for us. Because they are so passionately in love with God, the angels are perfectly conformed to his will. Whatever he tells them to do they do. Whoever he loves, they can't help but love. Because God cares for us so deeply, we can claim the wonderful friendship of angels.

What a tremendous encouragement to know that we are surrounded on every side by loving and powerful protectors. Thinking of angels can ease our sorrows, strengthen our faith, and lighten our hearts. G. K. Chesterton once quipped that "the angels can fly because they take themselves lightly." Of course the angels take themselves lightly. They keep things in perspective in a way that we can't. After all, they live in the presence of God himself. Their vision is clear, unclouded by the confusion and doubts we suffer. Neither do they fall prey to the insidious sin of pride, which weighs us down and chains us to our own small vision of the world. As we learn more about angels and their service, we will learn more about God. Our appetite for the spiritual life will increase and our longing for intimacy with our Creator will grow.

The time has come to open the gift and catch a glimpse of these powerful spiritual beings. Spend a few moments each day with the angels and ask God to use them to show you how lovingly and tenderly he cares for you.

Invite an Angel to Dinner

*I charge you, in the sight of God and Christ Jesus and the elect
angels, to keep these instructions without partiality.*

—1 Timothy 5:21

The Apostle Paul is reminding his disciple Timothy that we live our lives under the eye of heaven. We may think that no one sees us when we act in private, but in reality, we live in the presence of God and the host of heaven.

As a child, I had a keen sense of the supernatural dimension of life. I was fully convinced, because my parents told me I should be, that God was everywhere and that he was sometimes accompanied by angels. This conviction presented particular problems at bath time. I worried that I was not really alone as I splashed happily in the tub or as I undressed for bed at night. I was glad for God's company but embarrassed that he might be around at indelicate times.

These were childish concerns, of course. But there was something healthy about my acceptance of the fact that life did not end at my fingertips. A world existed that I could not touch or smell or see, yet I knew it was real. As I grew older, my child's worldview narrowed to an adult's, and it was some time before I understood once again that life was brimming with supernatural possibilities.

What would our daily life look like if it were infused with a sacramental understanding of reality? If we realized that the boundaries between heaven and earth are more like gossamer than steel? Would we so easily criticize and degrade one another if we knew that the angels were listening? Would we nag our children to death? Would we sulk whenever we failed to get our way? If we really believed that God knows what goes on in every home and every heart, wouldn't it make a difference?

I say this not to encourage us to "be on our best behavior" or to try to play-act before God. It simply isn't possible. But knowing that God is present, we might want to ask ourselves how he would view the situation. We might plead for his help to stop an angry outburst before it happens. We might rely on his grace more.

God isn't looking at us with a frown on his face, monitoring our behavior and marking every infraction in his rule book. Instead, he stands ready with his angels to help us become more like his Son. When you sit down with your family for dinner, remember that God will be there. No matter how chaotic your evening mealtime might be, ask yourself whether you might be entertaining angels. Perhaps there are a couple sitting nearby, ready to pass along an extra helping of grace just when you need it most.

> *Lord, restore to me the innocent wisdom of my childhood. Take away the blinders that keep me from seeing that life is so much more than meets the eye. Then part the curtain, just a bit, and give me a glimpse of your angels at work behind the scenes.*

Angels in the Storm

The angel of the Lord encamps around those who fear him, and he delivers them. —PSALM 34:7

*S*ometimes angels camp in the strangest places—like on the fender of a car in the midst of a nasty winter storm. . . .

Ann Shields was planning to drive from a small town in eastern Ohio to Lewistown, Pennsylvania, a journey of some four-and-a-half hours. Listening to the weather reports did nothing to ease her anxiety. The snow that was steadily falling would form a treacherous blanket over the icy mountain roads ahead.

"Father, send your angels to protect me," she said aloud as she turned the ignition key. Suddenly, she sensed there were two very large angels sitting on the front fenders of her car.

"I couldn't actually see them," she explained later, "but I was positive they were there—huge, young, and powerful, one sitting on the right and the other on the left fender. Through the entire journey, I got the feeling that they were talking and joking back and forth, wondering why they had been sent to watch over my little yellow Ford Fiesta in the midst of a Pennsylvania snowstorm. It must have seemed like a 'peanut operation' to them, but they seemed glad to do whatever God had asked. The whole way I felt tremendous peace, the kind of peace that honestly does surpass understanding. Normally, driving through that kind of storm on mountain roads would have been a white-knuckle affair for me, but this trip was sheer pleasure. The minute I pulled into the driveway in Lewistown, the angels disappeared."

Who knows why God sent not one, but two very powerful angels to maneuver a small car through a winter snowstorm? The angels didn't seem to know. It may have been one of their easier assignments. But God had his reasons.

Whatever they were, Ann Shields knows that God cares about her no matter what kind of trouble she's facing. And maybe that's the point of it. Many of our problems may be "peanut-sized" affairs when viewed from the perspective of heaven, yet the Father cares about them and about us. No matter what we face, he has plenty of power to spare, especially when it comes to taking care of his children.

Father, you know the anxieties and fears that often plague me. Sometimes even I know these are small matters in light of eternity. Yet I still can't stop worrying. Change me, Lord, and send your angels to give me joy and to convince me of your faithful care.

What Only Angels Can See

For I tell you that their [the little ones'] angels in heaven always see the face of my Father in heaven.

—MATTHEW 18:10

*T*he Bible tells us that no human being can see the face of God and live. Moses, whose relationship with God was one of extraordinary intimacy, begged God to show him his glory. But God replied, "You cannot see my face, for no one may see me and live. . . . You may see my back; but my face will not be seen" (Exodus 33:20, 23). Even so, when Moses talked with God, his own face shone so brilliantly that he had to cover it in the presence of others. His fellow Israelites could not bear even the reflected glory of God.

We can only imagine what it must be like to see God's face—to accurately perceive his beauty, his incredible power, his holiness, his love, and his majesty. Different ones of us vary in our capacity to see God, but none of us yet have the ability to know him as he knows us. It's as though God is telling us that it's still too dangerous. It would be like trying to pour Niagara Falls into a tiny thimble. The thimble would be utterly crushed and destroyed. This side of eternity, we are yet too full of distortions, sin, and frailty to look God in the eye.

Yet Jesus tells us that these angels continually enjoy this face-to-face communion with God. Maybe that's why they make such great guardians. They know how overwhelmingly attractive

God really is, and they are not seduced, as we are, into making idols out of lesser desires. They see the foolishness of choosing anything less than God. The things that tempt us do not tempt them.

How can you cherish a lie when you live in the presence of truth? How can you become anxious about the future when you've seen how well things turn out? How can you try to control your own life and the lives of those around you, when you understand the depth of God's wisdom and the awesomeness of his power? Why would you choose fool's gold when you know where the mother lode is?

Lord, whenever I catch the merest glimpse of you I long for more. I want to feast my eyes on you. Purge my soul of its darkness, that no shadows will blind me to your presence. Open my eyes that I may see what angels see.

Ladder of Angels

He [Jacob] dreamed that there was a ladder set up on the earth, the top of it reaching to heaven; and the angels of God were ascending and descending on it. And the LORD stood beside him and said, "I am the LORD, the God of Abraham your father and the God of Isaac." —GENESIS 28:12–13 NRSV

One of my favorite television programs as a child was *The Twilight Zone*. Its eerie stories, packed with surprising twists and turns, always piqued my imagination. Each program told the tale of unsuspecting people who were about to embark on an extraordinary adventure. Without warning, they would find themselves in a different world, not unlike their own but somehow strangely different. They had crossed over into that territory of the mind known as the "twilight zone."

Jacob had a dream that transported him into his own version of the twilight zone. He was on his way to Haran, the hometown of his grandfather Abraham. When night drew on, he slept under the starry sky with only a stone for a pillow and dreamed of angels climbing up and down a ladder connecting heaven and earth. When he awoke, he was terrified and exclaimed to himself, "Surely the Lord is in this place—and I did not know it! This is none other than the house of God, and this is the gate of heaven."

The ladder in Jacob's dream symbolized the connection that exists between heaven and earth. The angels move up and down the ladder, bearing our needs to God and carrying his provision to us. Jacob's strange dream, however, awaited its full interpretation for hundreds of years, until Jesus said, "I tell you, you will see heaven opened and the angels of God ascending and descending upon the Son of Man." Hitherto, the link between heaven and earth had been damaged by our disobedience. In Jesus, it was fully repaired. He is the link, the ladder, the gate between the throne of God and his people on earth.

Astonishing as this is, it's not the end of the story. The infinite distance between heaven and earth, between a holy God and sinful human beings, has been bridged by a Savior who actually lives within his people. Incredibly, this means that the ladder to heaven exists, not in some faraway place, but right inside our own hearts. If we belong to Christ, we can echo Jacob's surprise and exclaim about our own souls, "How awesome is this place! This is none other than the house of God, and this is the gate of heaven."

Father, your love for us is so passionate that you couldn't endure the pain of being separated from us. So you devised a plan to open the door to paradise once again. Thank you for giving me the gift of life in your Son, Jesus, the One who lives inside my soul. Help me to honor his presence within me. As I do that, draw near to me through the power of Jesus and the love of your angels.

The Angel and the Oatmeal

Even the sparrow has found a home, and the swallow a nest for herself, where she may have her young—a place near your altar, O LORD Almighty, my King and my God. Blessed are those who dwell in your house.

—PSALM 84:3–4

Jeanne Phelan was only three years old when she and her brother Jimmy began their search for a new home. With troubles enough of their own, her parents had reluctantly placed them in foster care.

One day Jeanne arrived home from kindergarten and found a shiny, new bike waiting for her. She could hardly believe it. "My foster parents met me, smiling and urging me to ride it. I told them I couldn't wait to show Jimmy. Suddenly their smiles froze. Fear crept over me. Jimmy! Where was Jimmy? I ran into the house and up the stairs into his room. My brother with the tousled hair and the teasing blue eyes, my only link to home and family, was gone. My foster parents had placed him in a home for boys. The bike was a gift to smooth things over.

"That evening, the smell of meatloaf drew me to the dining room table. As I began to eat, I couldn't stop wondering what Jimmy was having for dinner. I began to feel dizzy. Nausea pushed it's way up my throat and forced me to the bathroom. A vicious cycle of eating and vomiting ensued. Every morning my foster mother would confront me with a sumptuous breakfast of eggs, bacon, toast, orange juice, and oatmeal. How I hated oatmeal! When I couldn't keep it down, she would become enraged.

"Things got so bad that she finally sent me to a Catholic girl's home. The morning she dropped me off, she told me I would never see Jimmy again. The nuns took one look at me and placed me in the infirmary. A few days later a smiling young sister stood by my bed. She told me that many people had been praying for me and that she believed God was healing me. She said it was important that I learn to eat well, and then she helped me get dressed and walked me to the cafeteria. There on a long table was a steaming bowl of oatmeal!

"I picked up my spoon but was once again assaulted by nausea. Then, suddenly I realized that someone was sitting next to me. Startled, I stared into the beautiful face of a tall, strong man who was wearing clothes that appeared to be made out of white light. Gingerly, I reached my hand towards the shining cloth but didn't feel a thing. Was this my guardian angel? He smiled and I felt immensely comforted. He told me that Jimmy was okay and that I shouldn't worry. The angel also told me I didn't need to be afraid to eat. As he spoke, warmth flooded through my body. I grabbed my spoon, devoured the oatmeal, and ran to the kitchen to ask for more. After I finished eating, the young man disappeared, and I never saw him again.

"I never told anyone about the angel. I couldn't bear to be robbed of my joy through someone else's disbelief. That day I knew that the Father of the fatherless had swept into my life and that he would care for me. Talking to God became as natural as breathing. A while later I was even able to visit Jimmy. He was finally being adopted. I had memorized every freckle on my brother's face, so dear was he to me. But I was no longer afraid to live without him. God would watch over me so much better than any big brother ever could.

"To my joy, I was later adopted by a couple who provided a loving, nurturing home for me. That day with the angel was the turning point of my life. No longer was I a little girl without family and friends. I had an angel to watch over me and a Father in heaven who would never fail me or forsake me."

Father, you care about the widow and the orphan, and are a father to the fatherless. Thank you for your tender love. When I am tempted to feel alone and abandoned, help me to remember that you are near with your angels to watch over me.

Two

❧

Angels,
Now You See Them,
Now You Don't

Angels don't submit to litmus tests, testify in court, or slide under a microscope for examination. Thus, their existence cannot be "proved" by the guidelines we humans usually use. To know one, perhaps, requires a willingness to suspend judgment, to open ourselves to possibilities we've only dreamed about.

—JOAN WESTER ANDERSON, *WHERE ANGELS WALK*

hy do some people see angels while others see nothing? In one incident described in Scripture, a donkey sees an angel blocking the path ahead while its rider is oblivious to the angel's presence. Perhaps the answer lies with both God and us. First, the Lord has reasons we may never understand for opening the eyes of one person and shutting the eyes of another. Second, perhaps some of us have the kind of simple faith that invites the angels to show up.

One of my favorite pastimes as a child was to spend hours with my older brother and sister hunting for turtles. With nets in hand, we'd roam the lake on which we lived looking for pointy snouts to break the surface here and there. As soon as we spotted one, the chase was on. They were quick, but we were quicker.

Part of the problem with catching turtles is that they blend in so well with their natural habitat, making them difficult to see. But we loved these creatures and knew their habits and their hiding places. We told ourselves that we had developed "turtle eyes," the ability to see turtles where other people only saw reeds and logs and murky water.

I suspect that some people have developed similar skills when it comes to spotting angels. They've developed "angel eyes." They are sensitive to the variety of ways that God works in our world and are open to the possibility of miracles.

I confess that I have never actually seen an angel. But as I reflect upon my life, I sense the traces of their presence. As you read these brief meditations, take some time to think about your own life. Maybe, just maybe, the angels were at work and you didn't even know it.

An Army of Angels

Elisha prayed, "O LORD, open his eyes so he may see." Then the LORD opened the servant's eyes, and he looked and saw the hills full of horses and chariots of fire all around Elisha.

—2 KINGS 6:17

*S*ometimes we feel surrounded by trouble and difficulty, beset on every side by problems of one kind or another. This was the case with Elisha, an Old Testament prophet, who had angered one of the local kings. He and his servant awoke one morning to find themselves surrounded by an army intent on capturing them. They were outgunned, outmanned, and outmaneuvered. It must have looked like the last stand of Butch Cassidy and the Sundance Kid. But it wasn't.

Elisha's calm counterbalanced his servant's terror. He saw something no one else did. Though it looked like Elisha was outnumbered, his enemies were actually surrounded by a vast angelic host. Elisha prayed that God would open the eyes of his frightened servant so that he could perceive what was really going on— that God had planned a heavenly ambush to protect them.

Elisha's story tells us that some things can only be seen through the eyes of faith. But faith is something that does not come naturally to us. We want to taste, touch, and see for ourselves before we will believe.

A few years ago, a friend of mine was consumed by anxiety for her future. As she voiced her apprehensions, she said something that sums up our struggle to believe: "If I could only see what's going to happen, I could trust God for it." But the point of faith is that we need it *because* we can't see into the future.

My friend was making the same mistake I have often made. She was identifying faith with a certain kind of outcome. If things would work out as she hoped they would, then she would believe. But our faith will fail us if we tie it to a set of circumstances. It will become more like positive thinking than real faith. Instead, the faith that nourishes us involves trust in Someone rather than something—in the character of a God who is both loving and powerful enough to save us. God does not ask us to blindly trust him. Instead, he reveals himself through Scripture and through our own experience, to convince us that he is trustworthy.

God may or may not send an army of angels to rescue us, but we can be certain he will provide for us. We know that he sees around corners we don't even know exist. The more we trust him to provide, the more our faith will grow. We may not have supernatural visions of the kind that Elisha had, but we will develop keen spiritual insight as our faith increases. Angels or no angels, we will know without a doubt, that our God is faithful.

> *Lord, sometimes I wish you would hand me a crystal ball so that I could read the future. But I know you would much rather take me by surprise. Help me to realize that my security comes from placing my trust in you, not from knowing what's going to happen the day after tomorrow for the rest of my life.*

Sometimes Angels Don't Fly

It was no messenger or angel but his presence that saved them.
—Isaiah 63:9 NRSV

My father was a fighter pilot during World War II. He flew combat missions for the Air Force in Italy, France, and Germany. As a child, I enjoyed hearing that he had named his fighter bomber, a Thunderbolt P47, Sweetieface, his nickname for my mother, to whom he was engaged during the war.

A few years ago, he told me a story about his wartime experience that sent chills down my spine. It was April 1945 and the war in Europe was nearly over. He was leading an armed reconnaissance mission in central Germany when his squadron spotted an enemy airfield. They were later ordered back to the area to destroy the field, which they did with gusto.

"We bombed the hangars and strafed the field until nothing much was left. So many aircraft were destroyed that day that our commanding officer nominated us for a presidential citation. To document the success of the mission, I was eventually sent back to the field with two other men to photograph the wreckage.

"Once on the ground we realized that a few of the planes were still in pretty good shape. One of these was an ME109 Fighter. We thought it would make a nice prize for the Air Force, so we decided to fly it back to our airfield. I climbed into the cockpit, but when I turned the ignition, nothing happened. The battery was dead, so we left the plane where it stood. Later, I discovered that it had been booby-trapped with explosives in the wheel wells. Had that plane started, I would have been blown to bits."

I couldn't help but think about how incredibly different things would have been had the battery worked that day. My father would never have returned; his five children (including me) would never have been born; my mother would have married another man; you would never have read this book. . . . It's hard for me to stop thinking about the implications. Thank God for a mechanical failure. Or was it a failure, I wonder. Had God himself preserved my father's life for all that was yet to be? You may call it a coincidence, but I believe it was Providence at work. It may not have been an angel, but then again . . .

Father, I marvel at how well you care for us. Thank you for watching over every member of my family—my father and mother, my spouse, my children. There isn't a moment in our lives when your loving eye does not see us. You even number the hairs on our head. Help me to remember that when I start to fret and worry over those I love the most.

Just a Coincidence?

Are not all angels ministering spirits sent to serve those who will inherit salvation?　　　　　　　　—HEBREWS 1:14

*T*hate to admit it, but I came of age in the late sixties and early seventies, a peculiar "wrinkle in time," when everything was up for grabs, including the moral values that had shaped my life from day one. Like millions of other college students, I was experimenting with new ideas, new relationships, and a new outlook on life.

In my search for fun and fulfillment, I headed west for a few months to "search for my identity." With three hundred dollars to my name, I embarked on a journey that was to shatter my naiveté and eventually lead me to Christ. But there were many adventures along the way.

One of these took place in San Francisco, where my traveling companion and I landed after several weeks on the road. We were waiting to meet up with another friend who was to arrive a few days later. By then, my three hundred dollars had shrunk to almost nothing. I couldn't even spare enough change for a paperback novel. To save money in that most expensive city, we were staying with friends of friends, who happened to be involved in things that stretched even my worldview.

We spent our first day in a crowded Laundromat, clearing up a backload of dirty wash. It was a dreary job, but somebody had to do it. Suddenly I noticed a small, stoop-shouldered man dragging a cart of books behind him. I spotted the old man through the window as he turned the corner and entered the Laundromat. He advanced steadily until he reached my friend and me. He came to the point right away. Would I like to have a few books, rejects from the Chinatown library? Surprised but pleased, I scooped up an armload, and then he was gone. He had spoken to no one but me and had left as soon as he'd handed me the books. It seemed odd at the time, but I was grateful for something to read at last.

As it turned out, those books were a lifesaver. I was so absorbed in reading them that I had little idea of what was going on in the rest of the apartment. As we pulled out of San Francisco and headed for Los Angeles, my friend described what I had been too absorbed to notice. It seems that a parade of people had been injecting some very big-time drugs in that apartment. Two years later, one of the friends we stayed with there died of a drug overdose.

After a short stint in Los Angeles, we arrived in Phoenix, where some friends shared the Gospel with me in a powerful new way. It was the beginning of my long road to conversion.

Had an angel walked into the Laundromat that day, with an ingenious method for keeping me out of trouble? Or was my encounter with the little old man simply a coincidence? I don't really know. But I do know that angels are "sent to serve for the sake of those who are to inherit salvation." And though I didn't know it then, I was on my way.

Father, there is no end to your creativity. You invent a million strategies to keep us safe. Thank you for drawing near to me even when I was yet very far from you. I'm grateful for your angels and for the hidden ways they've watched over me.

Angelic Adversaries

Then the LORD opened Balaam's eyes, and he saw the angel of the LORD standing in the road with his sword drawn. . . . The angel of the LORD asked him, "Why have you beaten your donkey these three times? I have come here to oppose you because your path is a reckless one before me."

—NUMBERS 22:31–32

*B*alaam had prophetic gifts. That's why the King of Moab had summoned him. He wanted Balaam to place a curse on the Israelites who were encamped nearby. On his way to the king, Balaam encountered a fierce angel who blocked his path. His donkey saw the angel, though Balaam didn't. When the animal refused to budge, Balaam kept hitting the beast to get him to move. Then God opened his eyes and the angel spoke to him.

This story tells us that angels sometimes block our path because we are heading in the wrong direction. That's what happened to me a few years ago. I was working to secure a business deal that a number of other companies were also pursuing. I tried everything I could think of, but one obstacle after another kept popping up. I was frustrated, but refused to give up. Persistence is one of my professional virtues. It is also one of my vices.

Finally, though, I did stop pursuing the matter. Later, circumstances made it abundantly clear that it would have been a mistake to proceed. I couldn't see it at the time, but I now believe that God was blocking the path to keep my company from getting involved in something that would have blown up in its face. Perhaps if I had asked him to show me what was going on, I would have wasted less time and energy. I simply didn't see the situation clearly. I thought I knew the best course of action, and I tenaciously pursued it.

Paul's first letter to the Corinthians puts it like this: "For now we see in a mirror, dimly, but then we will see face to face. Now I know only in part; then I will know fully, even as I have been fully known." In this world our vision is blurred. Without God's help, we cannot tell which direction to pursue. Unless he opens our eyes, we simply will not be able to see things as they are. We may even pray against the work of Satan, only to find that we are opposing God himself.

Perhaps you are feeling thwarted in some way. You may be involved in a relationship that is going nowhere, a business deal that has soured, a ministry that is fraught with trouble. How do you know if you are under spiritual attack or if an angel of the Lord is trying to tell you something? Rather than assuming you know what God's will is, stop and ask him for wisdom. Pray that he will help you discern what is really going on. Is this a situation that calls for endurance and perseverance, or is God trying to point out another direction for you or your ministry?

Resist the temptation to keep beating your particular donkey, to force him to tread the path you have chosen. Ask humbly for God to guide you, and he will show you if one of his angels is blocking the path ahead. If he is, you dare not risk going forward.

Father, you have eyes that can see to infinity while I cannot even envision what's around the next corner. Forgive me for the times I have stubbornly persisted in the wrong way. Make me more sensitive to your angels and to your Holy Spirit, so that I will at least have the sense of Balaam's donkey to stand still and listen, to allow you to turn me around and head me in another direction.

Was It Really an Angel?

There the angel of the LORD appeared to him [Moses] in flames of fire from within a bush. . . . God said, "Take off your sandals, for the place where you are standing is holy ground." Then he said, "I am the God of your father, the God of Abraham, the God of Isaac and the God of Jacob."

—EXODUS 3:2, 5–6

*S*ometimes the Bible describes God as an "angel of the Lord." This is the phrase used in Moses' encounter with the burning bush. In this case, God makes himself known. Some theologians believe that this phrase always refers to God, rather than an actual angel. Whatever the case, it raises a question we all would like answered: How do you know whether something is the work of an angel or of the Holy Spirit? The answer is that most of the time you don't know. But does it really matter? Angels, after all, merely carry out God's plans. They do so joyfully since their wills are one with God's, but he's the One with the big ideas. They simply see to the details.

The truth is that God has an infinite number of ways of caring for us. Quite often, he even chooses human beings rather than angels to convey a message of his love.

Briefcase in hand, the collar of his trench coat turned up against the morning chill, Mark stood waiting for a city bus. He couldn't shake the feeling that he was supposed to share the Gospel with someone on the bus that day. "Finally I shot up a quick prayer acknowledging that I was willing to try if only God would show me who to talk to and what to say," Mark explained.

"I sat down next to an elderly man who looked as though he'd seen better days. Try as I might, I just couldn't get the guy to talk. Finally, I pulled out a small New Testament and randomly opened it to Romans 5:1. Then I noticed that he held a pocket New Testament in his hands. I asked him about it, and he told me that someone had given it to him, with the suggestion that he investigate Christianity. I read the passage from Romans aloud: 'Therefore, since we have been justified through faith, we have peace with God through our Lord Jesus Christ, through whom we have gained access by faith into this grace in which we now stand.' We talked for a few moments longer about what it means to have peace with God. Then I gave him my phone number in case he had any questions. When we parted, the old man turned to me with a smile and said, 'Well, you really have brightened my day.'

"I was out that evening, but my wife fielded a phone call for me that neither one of us will ever forget. It was the man on the bus. 'I need to thank your husband for something he said to me today. At first I didn't want to have anything to do with him. I even thought he might be a federal agent. He looked so clean-cut, with his trench coat and briefcase. But then he pulled out that Bible. Do you know that I was on my way home to commit suicide?' he told Sarah. 'Your husband's words about God changed my mind. I owe him a great deal.'

"I was astonished when Sarah told me the story that night. I didn't have a clue about what was going through that man's mind as we sat side by side on the bus that morning. But God knew. He knows what's in all our minds. That day he gave me an inclination and the grace to follow it."

Mark had simply listened to an interior prompting, a gentle whisper from the Holy Spirit. He was willing to risk embarrassment on the chance that God had something in mind. Mark spoke of what God had done in his own life, and his words sparked in that desperate man a new hope and a reason to live.

Mark is as human as anyone I know. He didn't announce himself in a burning bush (or bus, in this case) or with a trumpet blast, but he was definitely a messenger sent from heaven, an angel of flesh and blood, ready to do God's will.

You and I may never see an angel, but we know that they exist and that they work unceasingly on our behalf. Whether God is at work through his angels, directly through his Holy Spirit, or through us, doesn't really matter. What matters is that God loves us and finds an infinite number of ways to reassure us of that love.

> *"I am a link in a chain, a bond of connection between persons. God has not created me for naught. I shall do good, I shall do his work. I shall be an angel of peace, a preacher of truth in my own place while not intending it—if I do but keep his commandments."*
> —JOHN HENRY NEWMAN

Three

Angels to Guard Us

Angels where'er we go,
Attend our steps whate'er betide.
With watchful care their charge attend,
And evil turn aside.
—CHARLES WESLEY

We live in a dangerous world. At any moment our future could be erased by a heart attack, an accident, or a knife in the hands of an intruder. Worse than our anxiety for our own lives is our concern for our children. They seem defenseless against a predatory world, and our power to protect them is often inadequate.

Fortunately, God has not left them or us without recourse. One of the ways he protects us is through angelic guardians. Though Christians differ as to whether each of us has been assigned a personal guardian angel, most agree that angels watch over us in one way or another.

In fact, Scripture is replete with the feats of guardian angels. They blind prison guards, enabling believers to escape. They break chains as though they were snapping rubber bands. They transport people from one place to another. They impart courage in a moment of terror. They confound armies with their fierceness. In the world today they often work in hidden ways to preserve a life, to protect a church, and even to save a nation. Always, they work to carry out God's will. Perhaps their greatest accomplishments have more to do with protecting men and women from spiritual rather than mere material harm.

When you are tempted to feel afraid, for yourself or for your children, remember that you have the advantage of angels, powerful supernatural beings who are constantly watching over you. Though you do not see them, they are standing by to place a loving arm between you and danger. Take a moment and ask God to increase your confidence in his provision and to help you cooperate with the angels so that they can take care of you with joy.

An Angel on Board

"For last night there stood by me an angel of the God to whom I belong and whom I worship, and he said, 'Do not be afraid, Paul; you must stand before the emperor; and indeed God has granted safety to all those who are sailing with you.' So keep up your courage, men, for I have faith in God that it will be exactly as I have been told. But we will have to run aground on some island." —ACTS 27:23–25 NRSV

Paul had been placed under arrest in Jerusalem after a riot broke out in the temple in opposition to his preaching. He was now aboard an Alexandrian ship bound for Rome, where he was to make his defense before the emperor. Soldiers were also on board to convey Paul and a number of other prisoners to Rome.

En route to a safe haven in Crete, where crew and passengers planned to wait out the dangerous winter months, the ship ran afoul a violent Northeaster. The storm was so ferocious that the entire cargo and the ship's tackle had to be thrown overboard to lighten the load. For several days the forbidding sky refused to reveal a hint of sun or stars.

Finally, when hope had become nothing more than a dead man's dream, Paul told the others about his encounter with the angel. Like them, Paul had been terrified by the storm. But the angel calmed his fears and assured him that God would fulfill his purpose for Paul: he would arrive safely in Rome, where he would appear before the emperor and witness to his faith. Not only that, God had granted safe passage to everyone on board.

The angel imparted new courage to Paul. In turn, Paul was able to encourage the others. He was certain that the outcome would be exactly as the angel had told him.

However, some of the crew members failed to share Paul's faith. A few days later they tried to jump ship in order to save themselves. The soldiers were little better. They planned to kill the prisoners in the event of a shipwreck, lest any escape.

Even so, events proved Paul right about the angel's words. Everything happened exactly as the angel said it would. The ship ran against a reef and broke apart, but every single passenger escaped to safety on the island of Malta. And Paul was later transported to Rome to plead his case.

Paul talks about his heavenly encourager as an "angel of the God to whom I belong." He knew that his life and his future belonged in God's own hands. The same is true for every man and woman who loves God. Like Paul, we can expect that God will provide supernaturally for us. When we find ourselves at sea, not knowing which direction to turn, or when we discover ourselves the victim of some kind of disaster or shipwreck, we can echo the psalmist's words: "I cry to God Most High, to God who fulfills his purpose for me."

For God does have a plan and purpose for each one of us, no matter how stormy our circumstances. Like Paul we can find courage in the word that God speaks to us. And as we grow in courage we can, in turn, encourage those around us. Perhaps the God to whom we belong will send an angel to stand by us in our time of greatest need.

My Father, sometimes I feel as though enormous waves will swallow me whole. I'm frightened and confused, and yet I know that you love and care for me. Even though my plans may fail and my circumstances may end in shipwreck, I know that I can cry out to you and that you will yet fulfill your purposes for me.

The Toddler and the Angel

For he will command his angels concerning you to guard you in all your ways; they will lift you up in their hands, so that you will not strike your foot against a stone.

—Psalm 91:11–12

When I was a teenager, I spoke like a teenager, I thought like a teenager, and I *drove* like a teenager. In fact, I loved driving my mother's Thunderbird convertible at top speed, both in town and on the highway. I was young. I was indestructible. I was foolish.

One July morning I pulled into the driveway of a friend's home. We had planned a day at the beach, and the weather was being terrifically cooperative. We were excited to get going as quickly as possible, to catch all the rays that were to be caught. She climbed in, and I was just about to gun the engine into reverse, in my characteristically enthusiastic way. Suddenly I heard screams and shouts issuing from the house next door. As I turned to look, I saw the neighbors running frantically in our direction.

The object of their distress soon became apparent. A blond-haired toddler, perched on a tricycle, had been blissfully clinging to the rear bumper of the Thunderbird, unaware of his peril. I could not possibly have seen him as I prepared to back out of the driveway. One moment later, and this little boy would have been crushed beneath the wheels of my car.

I have little doubt that this toddler's guardian angel was on duty that day. And perhaps my angel had a hand in things too. The horror of that moment would have haunted me for the rest of my life—to have been the unwitting cause of a young child's death. I have thanked God many times since that he spared me that particular sorrow.

Who knows how many times you may have been saved from some tragedy or other by your guardian angel? Some of our angels, it's true, have to rise to the occasion more often than others. My father, who has had his share of close encounters, thinks he may have worn out several guardian angels in the course of his life. (I suspect that his simply took a few well-deserved vacations, rather than opting for early retirement.)

The point, of course, is not to see who can make their guardian angels run fastest and jump highest. It's simply to thank God for his loving care for us, "for commanding his angels to guard us in all our ways."

Father, how many times have you saved me from some catastrophe that I didn't even know was threatening? How many times did you send an angel to my rescue without my suspecting it? Thank you, Lord, that you make your angels winds and your servants flames of fire, heavenly servants to keep us safe.

A Miracle in Johannesburg

"See, I am sending an angel ahead of you to guard you along the way and to bring you to the place I have prepared."

—EXODUS 23:20

*C*hris and Jan were in a crowded airport in Johannesburg, South Africa on a hot Friday afternoon. It had been a trying day. They had missed their flight to neighboring Zimbabwe and had been wait-listed for the next. Suddenly, tickets were issued and loudspeakers announced that the flight would be departing momentarily. All passengers should immediately proceed to the gate.

As they hastily gathered their things in order to board the flight, they found that hundreds of other hot and laden passengers were hurrying in the same direction. "There must have been a hundred people cramming down the swift-moving escalator, with a huge crowd coming right behind them," explained Chris. "In front of us was a short, plump Greek-looking lady carrying bags that were much too heavy for her. She was so loaded down that she couldn't hang onto the handrails.

"Suddenly, she fell backwards on the steps of the escalator. She couldn't possibly get up by herself and, though we tried, we couldn't help her. Things were happening very rapidly. In a moment this poor lady would reach the bottom of the escalator and the rest of us would pitch forward on top of her, crushing the life out of her. In turn, I knew that we and others might be crushed to death by the mass of bodies behind us. Jan and I both cried out, 'Lord, help us!' and the most amazing thing happened. Suddenly this stout woman literally floated in the air and stood up on her feet. Her bags were neatly by her side, and we made it to our flight.

"Jan and I both sensed the angels had lifted her up. We know for a fact that what happened was a supernatural event. We cried out to God and he heard us. He saved many lives that day, including ours."

The Bible tells us that the Lord holds us in the palm of his hand, that underneath are the everlasting arms of a mighty God. In the frenzy of that experience, Chris and Jan never got to talk things over with the woman who had been lifted to her feet. If they had, perhaps she would have described strong arms holding her and sending her safely on her way.

Father, I never know when an ordinary situation may suddenly turn threatening, but you do. Whether my peril is physical, spiritual, or emotional, I know that your strong arms and the arms of your mighty angels are there to hold me up when I am too weak to stand. Thank you God, for raising me whenever I fall.

Unchained by an Angel

The night before Herod was to bring him to trial, Peter was sleeping between two soldiers, bound with two chains, and sentries stood guard at the entrance. Suddenly an angel of the Lord appeared and a light shone in the cell. He struck Peter on the side and woke him up. "Quick, get up!" he said, and the chains fell off Peter's wrists. —ACTS 12:6–7

*I*f you have ever been to Rome, you may have visited St. Peter in Chains, a church which claims to display the chains mentioned in this passage. Whether these are Peter's chains I couldn't say. But this church reminds us that Peter really was freed by an angel while under heavy guard in Jerusalem.

Shortly before Peter was arrested, King Herod Agrippa had put the apostle James to death. The people seemed pleased by this execution, so Herod grew bolder and arrested Peter. He handed him over to four squads of soldiers who were to guard him night and day. When the believers in the city heard the disastrous news, they prayed fervently for Peter's release.

One night, while Peter was sleeping, flanked on either side by guards, his angel came and nudged him awake. The next day Peter would have been brought out to the people, presumably for execution. But now the chains literally fell off Peter's wrists, and he walked out of prison and into the city a free man.

It took only one guardian angel to hoodwink four squads of soldiers who were standing guard. Herod became so infuriated when he heard about Peter's escape that he executed the guards.

Peter, himself, could hardly believe what had happened. He went straight to the house of some believers in the city. What occurred next is one of the more humorous incidents related in the New Testament. When Peter knocked on the door, a maid named Rhoda answered. She was so excited to see him, that she left him standing at the door and ran back to tell the others, who promptly told her she was out of her mind. They had prayed for Peter, but they could not believe that God had really answered their prayers. Meanwhile, the fugitive Peter stood on the steps desperately hoping that someone would let him in.

From Peter's story, we learn that our angels possess far greater power than the powers of evil that threaten us. We also learn that God heard the prayers of his people, despite their little faith. God had a plan for Peter and for his people that would not be subverted by any evil plan of his enemy. He allowed James to suffer a martyr's death. But Peter he spared for another purpose, through the ministry of an angel.

The gospel is in chains in many parts of the world today, and many believers suffer as a result. We need to pray especially for those who are heralds of the Good News, that God will send his angels to open prison doors so that many more people might come to know his mercy and his forgiveness. No matter how strong the opposition, God can send powerful angels who with a touch can overcome all resistance.

Lord, I know that many of your people are suffering and being martyred for their faith all over the world. I pray that you will confuse and confound every earthly and spiritual tyrant who attempts to suppress the Good News. Send your angels to empty out the prisons where my brothers and sisters are held and enable them to preach your Word with even greater power.

The Angel and the Computer

"When we cried out to the LORD, he heard our cry and sent an angel." —NUMBERS 20:16

*G*ary Gibson grew up believing in angels. As a child, he was pretty sure he even had his own guardian angel, who protected him on numerous occasions, particularly that time when snow and ice brought down a huge piece of slate roofing, narrowly missing him as it fell.

When Gary was only seven, he decided his angel needed a name. Gary explained, "My two favorite names were Raymond and Paul, but I couldn't decide which of these was right for my angel. Finally, I concluded that I should just call him Raymond Paul. So Raymond Paul it was from then on.

"Years went by and I forgot all about my guardian angel. I believed in God but didn't think much about the angels. One day last year it all came back to me.

"I work for a data processing firm which maintains computer files for various companies. One of our clients had rather urgently requested a personnel record for a certain employee. We didn't know the employee's name, only the employee record number. But that wasn't a problem since we could search for the record with the number. Hard as we tried, though, we just couldn't find it.

"Finally, my boss told us that no one could go home that night until we found the missing record. I had tried every bright idea I could think of but nothing worked. Finally, I did what I should have done at the start. I prayed. I asked God to show me how on earth to find that record.

"Suddenly, I had an idea about how to search for it. Most people were using a report writer program to look for the missing record. I decided to scan the file directly instead of using the program. Bingo! The record popped up on the screen. The whole place went nuts. Finally we could all go home.

"Imagine my surprise when I noticed the name next to the employee number. I could hardly believe my eyes. The person whose record we had been looking for was named none other than Raymond Paul!

"You can call it a coincidence, but the odds for something like that happening are astronomical. I believe it was my guardian angel's signature, his way of assuring me that God had heard my prayer and that he was still there looking out for me, ready to come to my aid whenever and wherever I needed him."

Lord, stories like this remind me that you move in mysterious and wonderful ways. Thank you for honoring the simple faith of children and adults and for showing me that no request is too small or too difficult for you to handle. Next time I need help, remind me to pray as a first rather than a last resort.

Four

❧

Angels with a Message

It is the province of knowledge to speak
and it is the privilege of wisdom to listen.
—OLIVER WENDELL HOLMES, SR.

ngels carry out a variety of supernatural roles in the structure of the universe. Their favorite seems to be that of messenger. In fact, the most frequent mention of them in the Bible is as messengers. The word *angel* derives from the Greek *angelos*, which in turn translates the Hebrew *mal'ak*, meaning "messenger."

The angels aren't merely heavenly mailmen, carrying love letters, special offers, and dunning notices from heaven to earth. Their role has much greater dignity. More like ambassadors than message boys, they represent the very presence and intentions of God himself.

Perhaps that's why they often seem to terrify people, who experience the same kind of awe that they might in the presence of a Holy God. Frequently the angel's first words are "do not be afraid." The angel Gabriel, whose primary role seemed to be that of messenger, told both Mary and Zechariah not to be afraid when he told them about the forthcoming births of Jesus and John the Baptist.

Do the angels still speak? Or are they silent now that the canon of Scripture has been closed? Certainly, angels can neither add nor subtract to the revelation of the Bible, but I believe they still convey messages from heaven to earth. Often, what we think of as mere coincidences may really be aspects of providence at work in our lives.

Remember the time you failed to notice an oncoming car until it was nearly too late? What caused you to look up just in time? Or perhaps a friend called not knowing that you desperately needed to hear from her. Maybe someone else said something that addressed a secret need in your life. Could the angels have been speaking, whispering a message from God himself?

If we have ears to hear, God will surely speak to us, and sometimes he will even use an angel to tell us of his mercy and guide us along the way.

An Angel and Two Miracles

"Greetings, favored one! The Lord is with you. . . . Do not be afraid, Mary, for you have found favor with God."

—LUKE 1:28, 30 NRSV

With these startling words, the angel Gabriel announced to Mary that she would give birth to a son who would inherit the throne of the great King David.

Not long afterward, Mary visited her cousin Elizabeth, who lived in the hill country of Judea. It was a meeting of opposite miracles—a young girl who had conceived a child without ever having slept with a man and a barren old woman whose womb had suddenly swollen with life.

Elizabeth's greeting rang out to Mary, "Blessed are you among women, and blessed is the fruit of your womb."

How strange and wonderful, to be called "favored" by an angel and then "blessed among women" by Elizabeth, the barren one who herself had been labeled "unblessed" all her married life!

Yet I wonder if these greetings came back to haunt Mary years later. Did the terrible irony of these words "blessed are you" pierce her soul as she watched her son lurch through Jerusalem, carrying his cross to Calvary, the hill of his unspeakable agony? Did the angel's promise that her child would be called the "Son of the Most High" ring mockingly in her ears as she stared at the bitter notice nailed to the wood above his head: "Jesus of Nazareth, King of the Jews"?

Was she tempted to think, "If this is what it means to be blessed, I don't want your blessing, God!"

We don't know. The Scriptures are silent. We can only imagine. Yet we do know that Mary was found with the disciples in the upper room when the Holy Spirit descended upon them like fire. Like them, she was praying and seeking God, no doubt searching her own soul but still clinging to his promises.

Mary's tenacity in the face of confusion, anxiety, disappointment, and terrible grief can be a source of comfort and strength. Have you ever received a message from God, a promise or a blessing, only to find that his definition of blessing or his timing and yours were out of sync? Mary may have wondered, as you have wondered, whether she really heard God or only imagined it. Perhaps she thought she had entertained delusions of grandeur. Why would God send an angelic messenger to her, a nobody from Nazareth? Yet she knew that he had.

You may have sensed the presence of an angel, whispering to you of God's love and his faithfulness. Resist the temptation to let go of whatever God has said to you through his word. Admit that you may not fully understand what he has spoken or promised, but ask him to show you and to give you faith as his word unfolds. Don't become discouraged if you don't feel blessed right away. Have faith in the Father and in his timing. It isn't naive to say that his timing is perfect. It's the simple truth.

Remember that Satan will throw God's promises in your face at the most inauspicious times. He'll challenge your belief that God really does love you just when you're feeling you can't stand yourself. He'll try to sow seeds of doubt in your mind in order to undermine God's word. Don't let him. Practice the tenacious faith of Mary, of Elizabeth, of Jesus himself. If you do, you may indeed suffer for a time, but you will surely receive great blessings from a gracious God.

> *Father, sometimes it seems as though you're making a story out of my life that doesn't make sense. Things haven't turned out as I had imagined and hoped. I confess I'm disappointed. Still, I know that I haven't read the end of the story you're writing. You know what you're doing, Lord. Increase my faith and let the plot unfold.*

Never Doubt an Angel

Then an angel of the Lord appeared to him [Zechariah], standing at the right side of the altar of incense. When Zechariah saw him, he was startled and was gripped with fear. But the angel said to him: "Do not be afraid, Zechariah; your prayer has been heard. Your wife Elizabeth will bear you a son, and you are to give him the name John."

—Luke 1:11–13

The angel Gabriel must have been used to frightening people. In this case, he scared the wits out of John the Baptist's father.

Zechariah and Sarah had been praying for years for a child, seemingly to no avail. Now, during Zechariah's priestly service in the temple, an angel appeared to him and stood near the altar of incense. In Scripture, incense symbolizes prayers ascending to heaven. The angel was standing near the altar on which the prayers of the Jewish people were offered to God. So it is fitting that Gabriel announced the answer to Zechariah's prayer in this way. For God had heard not only the prayers of this childless couple, but of all the Jews as well. The promised son would be a forerunner of the Messiah, the one who would liberate the Jews from their bondage.

Zechariah's reaction always amazes me. Even though he was terrified of the angel, he had the chutzpah to doubt the angelic message: "How do I know if you're telling the truth? Elizabeth and

I are much too old to have children." The presence of a spectacular angel wasn't enough to convince this skeptic. He wanted proof positive. Instead, he was punished for failing to believe Gabriel. The angel made him mute until the son he had promised would be born.

Have you ever prayed for something very difficult to believe in? In your heart, you doubt that God can or will do what you are asking. Even when God says yes, the doubt in our hearts often becomes apparent. Instead of erasing the last vestiges of unbelief, we cling to it, like Zechariah did.

God has already promised us many things in the Bible. He tells us that he loves us and that he forgives us, that there is no sin that Jesus cannot save us from. Think of the worst sin you can imagine. Chances are you read in the paper today about someone committing that sin: a woman who murdered her husband's lover, a minister who molested children, a dictator who slaughtered thousands of his own people, a serial murderer who preyed on women. Jesus died to save people like that. If that's true, why do we have such a hard time believing that God can forgive the kinds of habitual sins that many of us are guilty of: irritability, gossip, masturbation, unkindness, cowardice, defensiveness, self-concern? We pray earnestly for forgiveness, yet we cling to our disbelief. God couldn't possibly forgive us. We set ourselves up as judges of what it is and is not possible for God to do.

The encouraging thing about Zechariah's story is what he did with his tongue once his speech was restored after his son John was born. Rather than using it to challenge God's promise, he used it to praise him with this wonderful prophecy: "And you, child, will be called the prophet of the Most High; for you will go before the Lord to prepare his ways to give knowledge of salvation to his people by the forgiveness of their sins. By the tender mercy of our God, the dawn from on high, will break upon us."

Through the silent months, Zechariah's faith grew like a fruit to ripeness. And though the child he held in his arms was as yet only a seed of the promise, he no longer doubted the reliability of God's word. Instead, he proclaimed the message of God's mercy to any who would listen.

Lord, sometimes I wonder if I'm "believing impaired." I pray earnestly for something to happen but can't really believe that you will answer me favorably. Perhaps, like Zechariah, I'm so stubborn in my unbelief that an angel would have difficulty convincing me. Father, forgive my intractable skepticism and open my soul to the risks of faith.

A Sky Full of Angels

There were shepherds living out in the fields nearby, keeping watch over their flocks at night. An angel of the Lord appeared to them, and the glory of the Lord shone around them, and they were terrified. —LUKE 2:8–9

*I*magine the shepherds' astonishment to look up and see the night sky peppered with angels. Luke's Gospel tells us that the first angel was suddenly joined by "a great company of the heavenly host." The angels didn't announce the good news of Jesus' birth to any of the prominent people of Israel. They didn't appear to the mayor or the chief of police or even to King Herod in nearby Jerusalem, but to shepherds, plain men who stood guard over their noisy charges in the fields.

So often in Scripture, we see that God is not impressed with the things that impress us. He seems to go to great lengths to drive this point home: his Son was born to an ordinary Jewish couple; Mary and Joseph were poor people; Jesus lived most of his life in obscurity. We are impressed that the King of the Universe was born in a stable. But think of the tremendous condescension that God had already displayed by planting the seed of divinity in the womb of a human being. The distance between God and his creatures is far greater than the distance between being born in a palace or being born in a stable.

The angels had a message to deliver and they must have known that it would take root best in the soil of humility. So they told the shepherds about the Good Shepherd who would one day save them from their sins. And the shepherds believed.

The story of the shepherds convinces me that God is irresistibly attracted to humble hearts. It's as though the law of gravity has its spiritual equivalent. An object thrown from a high building will speed on until it hits the ground. So it is with God's grace as it courses from heaven to earth, coming to rest finally in the hearts of lowly men and women.

Father, have I become too sophisticated to hear your voice? Please keep me from pride in its many disguises and help me to learn from those who are humble of heart. Make my own heart a place of clarity, where your word can take root and bear fruit.

An Angel and a Birth Announcement

A certain man of Zorah, named Manoah, from the clan of the Danites, had a wife who was sterile and remained childless. The angel of the LORD appeared to her and said, "You are sterile and childless, but you are going to conceive and have a son."

—JUDGES 13:2–3

What is it with angels and birth announcements? We have already seen how the angel Gabriel announced the births of Jesus and of John the Baptist. In this case, an angel appears to the mother of Samson, the long-haired strongman, destined to save Israel from the might of the Philistines. In each case, God sent an angel to herald the coming birth of a special child. In each case, the circumstances were next to impossible. Either the woman was a virgin, barren, or well beyond child-bearing age.

Often, the angels had the unenviable task of announcing the news to a skeptical parent-to-be. In Sarah's case, God himself told Abraham that his wife would bear a son. You can hardly blame the old man for falling down laughing at the news. It was like a headline out of *The National Enquirer*: "Baby boy born to a ninety-year-old woman!" What will they think of next?

God seemed to be making a point through these surprise announcements. He would fulfill his plan, in his way, in his good time. What was impossible for men and women was a simple matter for God. He would display his power by raising up deliverers for Israel from the wombs of barren women, or in one case from the womb of a virgin. He, the Lord, and he only, is the author of life.

Why did God go to such lengths, we wonder. Perhaps it was because he knew that fallen human beings would otherwise take the credit themselves. Unless the circumstances seemed impossibly bleak, his people would think they could handle life on their own. Their innate pride would not allow them to acknowledge their need for him and for his deliverance.

Sometimes God works in precisely this way in our own lives. The circumstances may look hopeless. We may have cried out to God for some need in our lives only to hear an echoing silence. Then, just when we are ready to abandon hope, God may bring something new to birth in our lives. The very thing we long for may be given us, not simply to benefit ourselves, but to bless others as well. We may sense that an angel is near to herald the news. When such things happen, we recognize that God is who he says he is—our deliverer, our shield, the author of life, the Lord who saves us.

God envisions the future in a way we cannot possibly comprehend. Like Samson's mother, like Sarah and Abraham, like Mary and Joseph, we can lift our prayers to God, confident that he hears us, knowing that he will answer us in his time and in his way. We may even chuckle a little, as Abraham did, when God makes us a promise that seems to good to be true.

Father, you know the prayer of my heart. You've heard it so many times, you must be tired of it. I know I'm asking you to do the impossible, but you've done it before, many times. Whatever you do, Lord, I will accept your answer. But if you choose to do the impossible, I'll make sure you receive all the credit.

A Snow-White Angel

An angel of the Lord came down from heaven and, going to the tomb, rolled back the stone and sat on it. His appearance was like lightning and his clothes were white as snow. The guards were so afraid of him that they shook and became like dead men. The angel said to the women, "Do not be afraid, for I know that you are looking for Jesus, who was crucified. He is not here; he has risen, just as he said."

—MATTHEW 28:2–6

Mary Magdalene and another woman had come to the tomb to anoint the body of Jesus with spices, according to the custom of the Jews. Mary, you may remember, had been a prostitute, a woman from whom Jesus had cast out seven demons. She had gathered with a handful of Jesus' followers at his crucifixion, watching the one she loved, his body arched in torment, nailed hand and foot to a Roman cross.

She stood, a witness in the darkness that had covered Jerusalem, a fitting pall for the shadows that filled her soul. Mary had known in her own flesh the transforming power of Jesus' touch. She had little doubt of the hell from which this one man's love had saved her. Now he was in need and she could do nothing for him. She must have heard the chief priests and scribes as they shouted, "He saved others; he cannot save himself. He is the King of Israel; let him come down from the cross now, and we will believe in him." Their taunts would have pierced her soul. She was one of those he had saved. Now who was there to save him?

No one, apparently. The Messiah was dead. The hope of the Jewish people had disappeared in one bloody day. Now there was nothing left to do but bury the dead. That's why she had come to the tomb. To do what needed to be done, no matter how deep her disappointment or how painful her grief. She followed Jesus when he had been alive. It seemed right to be near him in his death.

It must have been a wonderful assignment for the angel to proclaim the incredible good news to a woman whose heart was breaking. I wonder if the heavenly host gathered for an arm-wrestling contest beforehand to see who would get to roll away the stone and announce the news of Jesus' resurrection from the dead.

The guards posted at the tomb were terrified when they saw the angel, whose appearance was like lightening. They must have actually fallen over, because the Scripture says they "became like dead men." Dealing with the guards must have been like flicking ants off a picnic plate. No power on earth could suppress the good news that the angel had come to announce.

Mary's disappointment and grief must have given way to bewilderment and then to joy. Jesus had overcome the death inside of her, and now he had himself come back to life.

Sometimes we feel that, like Mary, we are living between the Crucifixion and the Resurrection. We believe that Jesus rose from the dead, but we fail to experience Resurrection joy, because we are still waiting for God to heal some area of our life. Or perhaps we worry about someone we love, a spouse, parent, or child, who has not embraced a life of faith. We know that Jesus has acted with saving power in our own lives, but he does not seem to act with this same power in the lives of those closest to us.

At such times, it may help to reflect on the sorrow and disappointment of Mary Magdalene. She knew that Christ had the power to save her, but his power did not seem strong enough to save himself from crucifixion. Yet she stayed close to him, even in death. The angel said to her, "I know you are *looking* for Jesus who was crucified." You may also be looking for Jesus, seeking a deeper assurance of his love and power. Keep looking and remember the angel's words, "Do not be afraid. He has been raised."

Jesus, what must it have been like to have seen your risen body, with the wounds still fresh upon your flesh? What kind of joy must Mary have felt when she finally encountered you in the garden, alive again? Lord, make Mary Magdalene's joy my own as I realize that nothing can separate me from you, "neither death, nor life, nor angels, nor rulers, nor things present, nor things to come, nor powers, nor height, nor depth, nor anything else in all creation."

Five

Angels to the Rescue

Bless the Lord, all his angels
creatures of might who do his bidding:
Bless the Lord, all his hosts,
his ministers who serve his will.

—PSALM 103:20 NEB

*F*ar more effective than fire or police protection, angels have been known to perform the most daring rescue operations—walking around in a white-hot furnace, clamping shut the jaws of lions, blinding the eyes of prison guards. The angels seem to be up to any task God assigns.

This tells us something about the incredible power they possess. Angels are able to terrify their enemies, put tyrants to death, move swiftly from place to place, take a variety of shapes, and do what is generally unthinkable and impossible for us. They are creatures of another order. Knowing this, we can be very glad they are on our side.

The Bible is full of rescue stories. Many times we see angels coming to the aid of faithful men and women, who refuse to compromise with the spirit of the age. They care little whether they are out of sync with the times but only that they are in sync with God. Often they are willing to spend their lives for the sake of the truth.

People like Daniel, who risked a night with lions, impress us with their courage, as they should. But such people are not meant to be rare among believers. Around the world today, many Christians are paying the ultimate price of faith, surrendering both their freedom and their lives. All of us will face challenges, the temptation to make "little" compromises that will make life easier and more pleasant. Standing firm against such things will cost us something, perhaps even a great deal. As we resist such pressures, we can be sure of God's protection. He may or may not rescue us from the difficulty we are in, but he will surely protect our souls from evil. The Father has multitudes of angels at his beck and call, and we can trust him to send them to our rescue at just the right moment. For the Lord "guards the lives of his faithful ones and delivers them from the hand of the wicked."

An Angel Speaks in the Wilderness

God heard the boy crying, and the angel of God called to Hagar from heaven and said to her, "What is the matter, Hagar? Do not be afraid; God has heard the boy crying as he lies there. Lift the boy up and take him by the hand, for I will make him into a great nation." Then God opened her eyes and she saw a well of water. She went and filled the skin with water and gave the boy a drink. —GENESIS 21:17–19

Hagar was a single mother who was homeless, jobless, and penniless. She had run out of food, out of water, and out of hope. It seemed that she and her child would die alone in the wilderness, with no one to mourn them.

You may recall that she was the Egyptian slave of Sarah. As Abraham's wife, Sarah had heard the incredible promise that God would bless her and Abraham with a child, who would be the first of countless descendants. Yet God's promise only made her laugh. How could she possibly bear a son when she was already on the wrong side of menopause?

Maybe God needed a little help to make this crazy promise come true. Perhaps he meant to give them a son through her slave, Hagar. So, with Sarah's blessing and encouragement, Abraham slept with Hagar, and Hagar conceived a son, Ishmael.

Later, against all odds, Sarah gave birth to her own son, Isaac. Not surprisingly, a bitter rivalry grew up between the two women. Sarah insisted that Abraham toss Hagar and Ishmael out into the cold, and he did just that, offering the unhappy Hagar only some bread and a skin of water to help her and her child survive.

Since there wasn't any low-income housing in those days, Hagar was forced into the wilderness, where she wandered until her meager ration of bread and water ran out. On the point of despair, she sat down at some distance from her son, Ishmael. The last thing she wanted was to have to watch her only child suffer an agonizing death.

Hagar wept the tears of an abandoned and frightened woman. She was so alone. A stranger in a foreign land, with no one to notice her grief, or so she thought. Suddenly, in the midst of nowhere, an angel spoke to her from heaven. Hagar must have wondered if she had lost her mind after being so long without food and water. Yet the voice was real. The strong and comforting words of the angel dispelled her fear. A strange, new peace came with the angel's message. God had a plan and a purpose for her and her son. He would make Ishmael into a great nation! God would provide.

Notice that the angel didn't swoop down from heaven, carrying a glass of celestial water. Instead, he opened Hagar's eyes and showed her a well from which she could draw water. Abraham had given her a flask of water, which soon ran out. But God gave Hagar and Ishmael a well—water that would keep them alive and slake their thirst day after day.

Perhaps you are a parent, single or not, struggling to make a way for yourself and your children in the modern wilderness of this world. You may be able to feed and clothe your children, but you worry about their safety. Will they fall victim to the lure of sexual promiscuity, drugs, and violence? If you are single, you may feel lonely and in need of a partner to help you through life.

If so, ask God to open your eyes to his provision for you and your family, just as he did for Hagar. If God hadn't spoken to her through the angel, Hagar and her son would have died of thirst a stone's throw away from a well brimming with water. Perhaps God will send an angel to show you just how close his provision is for you.

Most of all, it helps to remember that God is the only one who can give you everything you need. You may think you simply need the right relationship, the right job, enough money. But in the last analysis, these things are but temporary provisions, just as the bread and flask of water that Abraham offered Hagar. All of us need to come to the living water, to the well that is Christ himself, in order to draw nourishment that will keep us going for the rest of our lives.

> *Father, the longer I live the more frightening life can seem. Friends and family haven't always come through when I've needed them. The things I thought I could count on have failed me. I'm beginning to realize that you are the only one I can always lean on. If you don't provide for me and for my children, who will? Lord, surely you know the plans you have for me—plans for my welfare and not for harm, to give me a future and a hope. When I call upon you, I know you will hear me.*

"A Bonny White Man"

*For he will command his angels concerning you to guard you
in all your ways. On their hands they will bear you up, so
that you will not dash your foot against a stone.*

—PSALM 91:11–12 NRSV

One of the roles that angels play is to act as a kind of heavenly rescue squad. They often protect us from harm, both spiritual and physical. Sometimes these angelic rescues are obvious, but often they are not.

Samuel Rutherford was a seventeenth-century Christian who had an encounter with an angel. When Rutherford was a boy of five in Scotland, he fell into the village well. His frightened playmates ran to the nearest house for help. Several men and women rushed to the rescue, fearful that the boy had already drowned. When they arrived, they were astonished to find the bedraggled Samuel, dripping wet and sitting on a mound of grass, not far from the well. "A bonny white man came and drew me out of the well," the boy told them. The well was far too deep for the boy to climb out of by himself. The "bonny white man" was an angel. That shining figure saw to it that Samuel would live out every one of the days that God had allotted him. Had God not intervened, Samuel Rutherford could not have achieved his purpose in life.

What was that purpose? Rutherford grew up to become a famous leader in the Church of Scotland. He played a prominent part in preparing *The Westminster Confession* and is credited with having written the *Shorter Catechism*. He also wrote *Lex Rex (Law Is King)*, a book whose principles were picked up by the English philosopher John Locke. Locke incorporated these ideas into his own writing, and his fans included John Witherspoon, Thomas Jefferson, Benjamin Franklin, James Madison, and many other of America's founding fathers. These men extracted principles from Rutherford via Locke's writing that were to form the foundation of the new nation, principles like the three branches of government with each branch acting as a check and balance for the others.

"The bonny white man" had rescued a young boy, who would one day be used to play a strategic role in the church and in the founding of America.

> *Father, I know that you have created me for a special purpose that only I can fulfill. Thank you for preserving my life and guiding me along the way. Whenever I am in trouble, I will cry to you, to my God who fulfills his purpose for me.*

Angels in the Fire

Then Nebuchadnezzar said, "Praise be to the God of Shadrach, Meshach and Abednego, who has sent his angel and rescued his servants! They trusted in him and defied the king's command and were willing to give up their lives rather than serve or worship any god except their own God."

—Daniel 3:28

Nebuchadnezzar was the King of Babylon. Shadrach, Meshach, and Abednego were three young men from leading Jewish families who were made to serve in the king's palace after Jerusalem was captured by the powerful Babylonian army.

The problem began when the king erected a huge golden statue, 6 cubits by 60 cubits (as much as 10 feet wide and 100 feet tall). Nebuchadnezzar sent out word to all corners of the realm that his subjects were to worship the idol. The penalty for refusing was to be thrown into a blazing furnace, hot enough to incinerate even the coolest customer. So no one refused, no one, that is, but the three young Jewish men.

Nebuchadnezzar was enraged by their refusal and ordered the furnace to be heated to seven times its normal intensity. Shadrach, Meshach, and Abednego were bound and thrown into the furnace. It was so hot that the guards who threw the young men in were instantly consumed by the flames.

The king was astonished by what happened next. "Was it not three men that we threw bound into the fire?" he exclaimed to his counselors. "But I see four men unbound, walking in the middle of the fire and they are not hurt; and the fourth has the appearance of a god."

Four men walking in the white-hot flames. Of course one was an angel so powerful that the king described him as a god. The three young men had no way of knowing they would miraculously survive their fiery ordeal. They couldn't be sure God would send an angel, but they trusted him for the outcome. They refused to dishonor him by bowing down to an idol, and God sent a fireproof angel to protect them as they walked freely in the furnace.

Notice that they were bound when they were cast into the furnace. But the king saw them walking around in the midst of the fire *unbound*. God had sent an angel not only to keep them from burning to death but to unfasten their bonds. In the midst of trial and persecution they were actually set free. Their story tells us that even in the most desperate circumstances, God can preserve our inner freedom as well as our lives.

No one is likely to command us to kneel before a golden statue today. Our culture promotes more subtle idols that demand our allegiance: sexual icons, success at any price, lust for power, unbridled materialism. The old idols keep popping up, disguised for modern times. Resisting the temptation to give into these cultural idols often entails great personal sacrifice.

Consider the single man or woman who refuses to give in to the fires of sexual passion, or the husband or wife who resists the temptation to sacrifice family life at the altar of career, or the unmarried woman who hears the dreaded news that she's pregnant but who resists the pressure to solve the "problem" with a quick visit to the local abortion clinic.

None of these are easy choices to make. We will often suffer loss, fear, confusion, and pain in our quest to be faithful to what and whom we believe in. But as we trust God for the outcome, we will experience a new freedom. Perhaps an angel will even stand by our side in the midst of our distress, unbinding and protecting us from the devouring flames that threaten to consume us.

Lord, you know how hard it is for me to remain chaste when everything around me shouts the pleasures of intimacy with another person, regardless of whether I'm married to them. Sometimes, I'm tempted to think the price of following you is too high. Please give me the courage of these three young men to stand up for what is right no matter what it costs. Reassure me that as I do this you will make me a person who is truly free and full of joy.

The Angels vs. the Lions

When he [King Darius] came near the den, he called to Daniel in an anguished voice, "Daniel, servant of the living God, has your God, whom you serve continually, been able to rescue you from the lions?" Daniel answered, "O king, live forever! My God sent his angel, and he shut the mouths of the lions."

—DANIEL 6:20–22

King Darius was in a bind. He'd been tricked by officials in his kingdom who were jealous of Daniel's increasing influence over the king. They persuaded Darius to sign a document proclaiming a thirty-day period in which it would be illegal to pray to anyone except the king. The penalty for ignoring the royal command would be a bloody death between the jaws of lions.

Daniel heard about the new law but continued to pray to God and praise him three times a day, just as he had always done. To make matters worse, he prayed boldly, in front of an open window, as was his habit. Clearly, Daniel was anything but a pragmatist. He could simply have stopped praying for a few days. What's a mere month in light of a lifetime of faithful prayer? Or at least he could have been a little more discreet. Why did he have to pray in front of a window, facing toward Jerusalem? However, Daniel refused to turn his back on his God in order to worship the powers of this world. He must have known that even small concessions would have encouraged a greater repression of faith. The initial edict lasted thirty days. What would stop the king from making the order permanent once he got everyone used to the idea?

Despite his regard for Daniel, the king had no choice but to abide by the decree he had issued and to cast him into a den of ravenous lions. That done, Darius placed a stone over the den and sealed it with his own signet so that he would know if anyone moved the rock in an effort to rescue the hapless man.

After a restless night, the king returned the next morning and called out to Daniel to see whether, by some miracle, he was still alive. To the king's joy, Daniel replied that he was very much alive and that he had been preserved by an angel who had shut the lions' mouths.

Darius had rolled a stone over the lions' den, entombing Daniel with the raging beasts, and placing his signet on the stone. Yet an angel had pressed the lions' jaws shut and saved Daniel's life. Centuries later, religious authorities in Jerusalem would place a similar stone over the tomb of Jesus and seal it with a guard of soldiers to make sure no one would tamper with his grave. Once again, mere stones could not stop God's angels. For two angels appeared at the tomb of Jesus and addressed the women who came to anoint Jesus' body: "Why do you look for the living among the dead?"

Both Daniel and Jesus refused to compromise their faith. God preserved the one from death and caused the other to conquer death once and for all. We may not face the kind of persecution that was meted out in the ancient world, but we will surely face pressures to compromise our beliefs in order to fit in with the world around us. When that happens, remember Daniel and Jesus.

Remember that you can sell your soul by making the wrong kinds of compromises. Remember that God protects the blameless man or woman. And last of all, remember the angels.

Jesus, I need your wisdom to know when to stand firm and when to compromise. Sometimes I pride myself too much on being able to stand in the middle. But you were controversial when you needed to be. Lord, you know I am not looking for trouble, but help me to stand firm when trouble comes my way. Don't let "being nice" be my highest goal. Give me the courage to be faithful, regardless of the consequences.

The Greatest Rescue Ever

> *Then God said, "Take your son, your only son, Isaac, whom you love, and go to the region of Moriah. Sacrifice him there as a burnt offering on one of the mountains I will tell you about."*
> *. . . Then he [Abraham] reached out his hand and took the knife to slay his son. But the angel of the LORD called out to him from heaven, "Abraham! Abraham! . . . Do not lay a hand on the boy." . . . Abraham looked up and there in a thicket he saw a ram caught by its horns. He went over and took the ram and sacrificed it as a burnt offering instead of his son.*
>
> —GENESIS 22:2, 10–13

*S*omething about this familiar story both deeply disturbs and strangely comforts us. How could a loving God ask Abraham to kill his own son, the son that he loved? Worse yet, how could God require Isaac's life as a sacrifice? We know from how the story ends that God was testing Abraham. Would he give back to God the one thing most valuable in his life, the son God had promised?

We can almost see the sweat dripping from the father's brow, gray-blue veins bulging across his temples, his powerful arm extended over the flesh of his son, knife in hand, ready to make the dreaded sacrifice.

The boy was bound to the rock like an animal ready for slaughter. What could possibly have been going through Isaac's mind in that moment? Did he catch and hold his father's gaze?

What agony of love and bewilderment must have passed from father to son and back again.

Then, when all hope had fled, an angel called out from heaven. "For God's sake, Abraham—don't harm the boy!" The pain that had passed between father and son turned to wonder. Abraham must have quickly untied Isaac, wrapping him in his arms, the man's tears mingling with the tears of the terrified boy. Isaac would live. Instead of a boy, a ram. A hapless animal caught in a thicket would provide the required sacrifice.

We breathe a sigh of relief as we read one of the most famous last-minute-rescue stories in biblical history. We marvel at the tremendous faith of Abraham. We doubt we could ever do what he did. We are disconcerted that God would even pretend to want a man to sacrifice his own son.

Yet the story of Abraham and Isaac points to the greatest rescue story of all time. Our confusion turns to awe and gratitude as we realize: what God did not require of Abraham, he required of himself. In Jesus, God's only Son, the Son the Father loved, we recognize the ultimate sacrifice. The "ram caught in the thicket" actually hinted at what was to be. The ram prefigured Jesus and his substitutionary death on Calvary. It might surprise you to learn that Jesus was nailed to a cross perhaps a quarter mile from Mount Moriah, possibly the very place where Abraham was prepared to sacrifice Isaac.

Centuries before Jesus even came on the scene, the Father was hinting at his plan, an incredibly daring and loving rescue operation. He knew how radical a remedy was needed to heal our brokenness and bring us back to him. When we are tempted to feel that God is asking too much of us, it may help to recall what he asked of himself. We understand and empathize with Abraham's anguish, but do we ever consider the terrible price the Father paid? A moment's reflection will convince us that Jesus is the greatest gift of love the Father could have given us: "his Son, his only Son, whom he loved."

Father, I didn't realize the incredible price you paid when you gave your Son to me. I stand in awe of your mercy. Never let me doubt your love again or say that anything you ask is too hard to give. You gave me the One you loved the most, let me gladly surrender my soul and everything I am into your loving arms.

Six

❧

Angels on Fire
with Love

*The angels are pure spirits, the mighty Princes of Heaven who
stand before God, gazing on His unveiled presence. They are burning
fires of love, filled to overflowing with the plenitude of happiness.*
—PAUL O'SULLIVAN

ary Kinnaman, author of *Angels Dark and Light*, says that "next to God, angels are like flashlights on the surface of the sun." His point is that God's glory is infinitely greater than that of the angels. Even so, when confronted by a vision of an angel, we are tempted to bow down and worship. This happened to John, the author of the Book of Revelation. So overwhelmed was he by the angel who spoke to him that he fell at its feet in adoration. The angel quickly corrected John. "You must not do that!" he insisted. "I am a fellow servant with you and your comrades who hold the testimony of Jesus. Worship God!"

If angels pale in comparison to God, what does that tell us about the exquisite beauty of the Father, Son, and Holy Spirit? Rather than distracting us from God, angels can actually inspire our worship.

Unlike us, the angels in heaven can no longer be tempted to sin. Their wills have become one with God's own will. The philosopher Mortimer Adler acknowledges this when he says, "Once blessed, the good angels are confirmed in goodness. They cannot sin. Seeing God's essence, they cannot turn away." What a wonderful notion that is: to be *confirmed in goodness*, incapable of offending God. Those of us who belong to God will one day dwell in his presence just as the angels do. Then we too will be confirmed in goodness, and with that goodness will come perfect praise and joy unspeakable.

Angels Rejoiced

When God brings his firstborn into the world, he says, "Let all God's angels worship him." —HEBREWS 1:6

The writer of the Letter to the Hebrews makes it abundantly clear that angels worship Jesus as the firstborn of the new creation. Jesus is not simply a bit greater than the angels, but infinitely superior to them. Knowing this, the angels adore him.

John's Gospel says of Jesus, "He was in the world, and the world came into being through him; yet the world did not know him. He came to what was his own, and his own people did not accept him." I have always been struck by the irony of this passage. Only a handful of people even noticed that Jesus had come on the scene: the wise men, the shepherds, his parents, his cousins, the tyrant Herod, and Simeon and Anna. Everybody else missed it. The Creator had come incognito. The biggest news event in the history of the world went unnoticed, unreported, and uncelebrated by most of the people.

Sandi Patti sings a powerful song about the Resurrection, entitled "Was It a Morning Like This?" The song celebrates the living Christ breaking forth from the tomb. One of the lines goes like this: "Did the grass sing? Did the earth rejoice to feel you again?" We feel the exuberant joy of the risen Christ, that even "the stones cry out."

Somehow, we would like to sing this same song about Jesus' birth. It seems fitting that the earth would have thrilled the moment its Maker became incarnate. True, there were angels and a star of some brilliance that guided the wise men, and yet we know of nothing more spectacular: no earthquakes or floods or meteor showers to herald the event. There was no cheering crowd, no glitzy birthday bash, no front-page story in the *Jerusalem Post*.

Yet the angels were there. They knew exactly what was going on. They witnessed what the world would not or could not. And they shared the good news of his coming with the shepherds in the field.

Sometimes Jesus, for all his glory, is yet hidden from us. We become distracted by our unredeemed desires—for money, for relationships, for perfect health. Or we may feel bereft of his presence and power through no fault of our own. Though Jesus lives in us, we fail to recognize his presence in ourselves or others.

Like the sun behind the clouds, Jesus is a living reality whether we perceive him or not. Though sometimes hidden from us, he is not hidden from our angels. When we want so badly to sense that he is with us, let us take comfort in knowing that our angels perceive what we do not. Knowing this, we can pray that God will open our eyes and our hearts to his presence.

> *Jesus, the angels are privileged to stand in your presence. Help me to perceive the hidden ways in which you are present in my life. Open my ears so that I may hear you, even when you are only whispering. Open my eyes through faith that I might bow down and worship as the angels do.*

When Angels Worship

*"Holy, holy, holy,
is the Lord God Almighty
who was, and is, and is to come."*

—REVELATION 4:8

The Book of Revelation offers us a rare glimpse of the worship that takes place around the throne of God in heaven. We are even allowed to eavesdrop on the angelic song of praise, which "is uttered day and night without ceasing."

The angels show us that it is not possible to refrain from worshiping God once you have given yourself to him and really beheld his face. Unlike us, their worship is not hindered by a veil separating them from the One they love. They enjoy perfect communion, perfect love, perfect understanding, and perfect freedom. Though we "see through a glass darkly" and suffer confusion, fear, and doubt as a result of our clouded vision, the angels see clearly and proclaim the truth about God unceasingly. What is this truth? It is this:

- That the Father is holy; the Son is holy; and the Spirit is holy.
- That God is almighty: no one has more power than he does.
- That God is eternal: he always has been, he is now, and he always will be.

The angels show us that worship involves proclaiming the truth about God. When we are tempted to believe that God is other than holy—that he treats us as we sometimes treat others, unkindly or unfaithfully, let us remember the truth of the angels' song.

When we fear that God may not be strong enough to save us from our current predicament, let us repeat and believe with the angels that God is full of might and that his arm is not too short to draw us out of our self-created darkness and into the light of his presence.

When we doubt the eternal purpose of God, when we suspect that he acts capriciously, when we wonder why Christ seems to delay his coming—let us agree with the angels that God has always been faithful, that he is currently present and active in our lives, and that he is the One who will surely come to establish his reign for all time.

> *God, I confess that I have not always given you the benefit of the doubt. Because sin has distorted me and everyone I know, I have sometimes projected those distortions onto you. Forgive me for thinking that you are anything but loving, wise, all-powerful, and merciful. As I turn from false images of who you are, turn your face toward me, that I might begin to perceive the whole truth about you.*

The Burning Ones

Then one of the seraphs flew to me with a live coal in his hand, which he had taken with tongs from the altar. With it he touched my mouth and said, "See, this has touched your lips; your guilt is taken away and your sin is atoned for."

—ISAIAH 6:6–7

*I*saiah had a vision of the throne room of heaven: he beheld the great God surrounded by seraphim, magnificent angels with six wings, two to cover their faces in reverence, two to cover their feet in respect, and two to enable them to fly. In Isaiah's vision they called to each other and said: "Holy, holy, holy is the Lord of hosts, the whole earth is full of his glory."

If you think Isaiah was terrified by what he saw, you are absolutely right. He was sure he was a dead man, certain that no human being could see God and live. Fortunately for him, a seraph took care of the problem by taking a burning coal from the altar and pressing it against his lips. This symbolized the purifying action of God.

The seraphim are some of the more exotic angels described in the Bible. They live constantly in the presence of God, surrounding and guarding his throne and singing his praises. They are called "the burning ones," perhaps because they reflect God's holiness. I like to think it is because they burn with love for God. The picture that Isaiah paints is of a royal court in which the King is accompanied by a magnificent retinue of supernatural attendants.

It is good for us to read such passages in Scripture, though they seem so strange. As creatures of flesh and blood, it is often difficult for us to paint a very compelling picture of heaven. Partly because of this, we lose our sense of reverence and awe of God. We try to tame him for our purposes. We disregard his greatness, presume upon his goodness, and sometimes try to manipulate him into doing our will. And though the God of the universe beckons, calling us into his holy presence, we are often much too busy for him.

The angels must be scandalized. They know that God has invited us to share a wonderful intimacy with him, but wonder how we could possibly take that privilege for granted. They know what a terrible mistake it would be to lose one's fear and awe of the Mighty God.

Augustine says that "one loving soul sets another on fire." Perhaps that's what the angels can do for us. They can show us by example, as they showed Isaiah, what it means to live in the presence of God.

Try learning from the seraphim. Quiet your heart and imagine the scene in heaven. Ask God to give you a glimpse of his majesty. Beg him to purify your soul, like he did for Isaiah. Sing his praises and tell him how wonderful he is. Cover your face in reverence and bow down before him. Then, be like the angels, burning with love as you behold God's beauty, his power, and his loving-kindness. Think for a moment about some of the Lord's many names: Almighty, Ancient of Days, God of Israel, Only Wise God, Everlasting Father, I AM, Creator, Lord, Mighty God, Lamb of God, Lily of the Valley, Savior, Man of Sorrows, Messiah, Prince of Peace, King of Glory, King of Kings, Shepherd, Redeemer, Rock, the Alpha and Omega.

"Be still and know that I am God."

Who can begin to fathom your greatness, God? You are the Alpha and the Omega, the First and the Last. You are holy and full of light. You have loved me with an everlasting love. Forgive me and purify my heart. Help me to know my sin that I might know your mercy. Anoint my lips to sing your praises.

Higher Than the Angels

> *After he [Jesus] had provided purification for sins, he sat down at the right hand of the Majesty in heaven. So he became as much superior to the angels as the name he has inherited is superior to theirs.* —HEBREWS 1:3–4

Angels are everywhere in the New Testament, signaling a closer rapport between heaven and earth, established by the coming of Jesus. In fact, the angels couldn't seem to stay away from the man from Nazareth. Like parentheses encircling a phrase, they were present at both the beginning and end of Jesus' earthly life.

Notably, the angels were present at his ascension. Few of us stop to consider the significance of Jesus' reentry into heaven, an event that is mentioned in the Book of Acts and described elsewhere in the Bible. After the Resurrection, Jesus entered heaven as a victor. But that's not all there is to the story. By becoming human, Jesus was able to defeat Satan and release us from the terrifying bondage of evil. Having done that, the King of the Universe did not shed his human nature like a worn-out suit. Instead, he chose to reign forever as both God and man.

John Chrysostom touches on this incredible truth when he says that the angels looked on at the ascension because they wanted "to see the unheard of spectacle of man appearing in heaven." He goes on to say: "Today we are raised up into heaven, we who seemed even unworthy of earth. We are exalted above the heavens; we arrive at the kingly throne. . . . Was it not enough to be elevated above the heavens? Was not such a glory beyond all expression? But He rose above the angels, He passed the Cherubim, He went higher than the Seraphim, He bypassed the Thrones, He did not stop until He arrived at the very throne of God."

The heights to which Jesus has ascended and to which he invites us are dizzying. The angels look on with awe and so should we. Higher than the seraphim, more glorious than the cherubim, our God reigns!

> *O Lord, how great you are! When I consider the heavens, the work of your fingers, the moon and the stars which you have set in place, what am I that you should care for me? Yet you raise me up and give me a share in your eternal kingdom. How great you are, how majestic is your name in all the earth!*

A Love to Rival the Angels

Whenever the living creatures give glory, honor and thanks to him who sits on the throne and who lives for ever and ever, the twenty-four elders fall down before him who sits on the throne, and worship him who lives for ever and ever.

—REVELATION 4:9–10

Once again, we are transported to heaven, where angels surround God's throne and sing his praises: "You are worthy, our Lord and God, to receive glory and honor and power, for you created all things, and by your will they existed and were created."

Thomas Aquinas was one of history's great theologians. He was nicknamed the "angelic doctor," at least partly because he attempted a thoroughgoing study of the angels. Wise as he was, he had an experience of God toward the end of his life that convinced him to leave his great work, *Summa Theologica*, unfinished. When urged to complete it, he replied, "The end of my labors is come. All that I have written appears to be as so much straw after the things that have been revealed to me." Thomas was far more than a scholar. He was a man who rivaled the angels in his love for God.

We get an inkling of his passion from his own words: "The good God is that ravishingly attractive Being who is resisted only when he is not seen; he is infinite enticement, rapturous beyond a man's most extravagant desires, captivating lovableness to tear the heart out of a man. Confronted by divine goodness, the heart of man bursts into such a flame as to make a torch of his whole life. Fascinated by the invitation inherent in such goodness, a man finds no journey too long, no danger too great, no obstacle too wearying; here is strength, courage, daring for the weakest of men, for if this goodness be achieved nothing is lost, if this be lost everything is bitterly lost."

Aquinas shows us what is possible when a man or woman falls in love with God. Every other care recedes and one burning passion emerges. This kind of all-consuming love is a gift that comes only from the hand of God.

Why not ask God for this gift so that you can compete with the angels in your passion for God? You may not surpass them, but what joy you will discover in trying!

Father, you are infinite enticement, able to satisfy me beyond my most extravagant desires. May I be so consumed by love of you that my life will become a fire to praise you. If I have you, I have everything. If I lose you, everything is utterly and bitterly lost.

Seven

❧

Angels in Disguise

Art thou some god, some angel, or some devil?
—WILLIAM SHAKESPEARE, *JULIUS CAESAR*

With all this talk of angels, why isn't life more pleasant? The answer has to do with both the angels and with us. Life is often painful, confusing, and tragic because human beings have fallen from grace and turned their hearts from God. Bad as this is, that's not all there is to it.

Sometime before the dawn of history, God tested the faithfulness of his angels, and found some of them wanting. Lucifer, or Satan, is thought to have been one of the most majestic of the angels, a powerful being who failed the test because of his enormous pride. Tradition holds that with him fell a third of the angels.

However many angels failed the test, we know that there are more than enough to go around. As such, they war for the souls of men and women, seeking to consign as many to destruction as possible. Martin Luther acknowledged this peril when he said, "The devil is also near and about us, incessantly tracking our steps, in order to deprive us of our lives, our saving health, and salvation." Luther also knew that God's power is more than sufficient to defeat every enemy.

It isn't pleasant to talk about the devil and it isn't prudent to think about him too much, but we need to realize that not all the angels are on our side. The more we align ourselves with Christ in humility, faith, and obedience, the greater will be our safety and the stronger will be our confidence. The light will grow brighter and the darkness will diminish as God confirms his rule in our hearts.

An Insane Angel

How you have fallen from heaven, O morning star, son of the dawn! . . . You said in your heart, "I will ascend to heaven; I will raise my throne above the stars of God; . . . I will make myself like the Most High." But you are brought down to the grave, to the depths of the pit. —ISAIAH 14:12–15

This passage probably refers to the fall of the King of Babylon. Yet many biblical scholars believe that it also refers to Satan's fall, before the beginning of human history.

Satan, or Lucifer (meaning "morning star" or "light bearer"), incited a rebellion in heaven. He wanted to take God's place, to sit on his throne and lord it over the universe. Eventually his pride forced him out of heaven.

Yet Satan's attempt to take over was nothing but an act of madness. How could a mere creature ever take the place of the Creator? To understand how ludicrous his position was, remember, for a moment, that we commit people who think they are God to insane asylums. Or imagine what would happen to me if I suddenly started telling everyone in sight that I was the emperor of Japan. Of course, this is a ridiculous scenario, but Satan's attempt to overthrow heaven was equally bizarre. As John Stott points out, "The essence of sin is man substituting himself for God, while the essence of salvation is God substituting himself for man." Satan's pride blinded him to the folly of his desire and evil took root in his heart.

Though the devil may be insane, he is powerfully insane, and, as such, he can tempt us to lose touch with reality too. This happens whenever we prefer our own will to God's. We do this in obvious ways: by committing murder, adultery, or grand larceny. But we also do it in more subtle ways. We want God to grant us a favor, to get us a particular job, a date, a raise in pay. Or we plead for him to heal someone instantaneously. Essentially, we want God to be our tool—to do our bidding whenever we command. All the while, Satan stands by to tell us that we are making reasonable demands.

What's wrong with asking for such things, you ask. Nothing at all. Jesus tells us that we should. But we begin to lose touch with reality whenever we try to force God to do what we want. We pile anxious prayers, one upon another. We attempt to persuade God to do whatever we ask by striving to behave perfectly, by following all the "rules." Sometimes we even use fasting (a helpful spiritual discipline, in itself) as a means of controlling God and getting him to do what we want. We fret and stew when we don't think God is acting as he should. We conclude that he doesn't love us enough to answer a few simple prayers.

Perhaps God loves us too much to do everything our way. He knows how miserable life would be if millions of "little gods" were ruling their respective universes. Often, God does answer our prayers in ways that delight us. But sometimes the answer is no. When that happens, let us take a moment to acknowledge his goodness, to thank him that he is in control and that we aren't. Let us pray that God will protect us from the long tentacles of pride, which try to strangle our reason and persuade us that we always know what's best. As we do this, a deeper humility and greater sanity will grow in us. Our minds will be freed from delusions large and small and we will grow in wisdom and peace.

Lord, you are God and I am but your creature who loves you. You know everything and I know only the merest trifles. You are all powerful and I am weak and vulnerable. You are everywhere and I can only be in one place at a time. You created me out of nothing and I can't make anything that lives. Your love fills the universe and my love is but a flame that flickers. Father, what a great combination we are, like a hand and a glove—you in your strength and me in my weakness!

A Telegram from Hell

To keep me from becoming conceited because of these surpass-
ingly great revelations, there was given me a thorn in my flesh,
a messenger of Satan, to torment me. Three times I pleaded with
the Lord to take it away from me. But he said to me, "My grace
is sufficient for you, for my power is made perfect in weakness."
—2 CORINTHIANS 12:7–9

We have seen that one of the roles angels play in human affairs is to convey messages between God and human beings. Unfortunately, it seems that Satan likes to send messages of his own from time to time.

In the apostle Paul's case, we don't know what his "thorn in the flesh" was, his "messenger from Satan." All we know is that it came to him after he had a remarkable vision in which he was caught up into heaven itself. We know from what Paul says that God allowed the enemy to act as the messenger. Two verses later, Paul tells the Corinthians that he is content with "weaknesses, insults, hardships, persecutions, and calamities for the sake of Christ; for whenever I am weak, then I am strong." Any of these things could describe the "thorn" that Paul mentioned. Perhaps he left it deliberately vague so that you and I might realize that we too will have our "thorns," though our circumstances may differ from his.

You can be sure that Paul wasn't happy to receive this black telegram from Satan. So he pleaded with God, not once, but three times. "Please, Lord, take it away. It's from Satan. How can it possibly be good for me?" Paul didn't respond to his affliction by simply resigning himself to his fate. He took the problem straight to God, and God gave Paul an answer—not the one he wanted but the one he accepted. Satan had a message for Paul, but God had a deeper message. Whatever Paul suffered would provide a tremendous opportunity for him to actually become more powerful in Christ. In God's strange economy, power was perfected in weakness. His grace would cause Paul to be strengthened if only Paul would endure his trial patiently.

Perhaps you have received a few messages from Satan too, messages that frighten or discourage you or make you doubt God's love. The messages that come from below can arrive in a variety of ways: a tongue-lashing from your boss, a crippling disease, a catastrophe that strikes your family. The possibilities are endless. Perhaps God has permitted you or someone you love to suffer deeply. Plead to God to take your affliction away. Don't accept the lie that you deserve whatever bad things happen. But listen while you're in God's presence, pleading your case. For he might have a deeper message than the one Satan intends to deliver. God might have a secret he can share with you in no other way. Perhaps he will whisper a word that will help you make sense out of life and give you greater hope and confidence for the future.

Father, sometimes I am so confused about my life. Something difficult happens and I wonder if you're punishing me. I become fearful, tense, and confused. But then I remember who the "author of confusion" really is—my enemy and yours. Lord, I ask you to protect me and help me to pierce through this present darkness to understand what's really going on.

A Case of Possession

They sailed to the region of the Gerasenes, which is across the lake from Galilee. When Jesus stepped ashore, he was met by a demon-possessed man from the town. For a long time this man had not worn clothes or lived in a house, but had lived in the tombs. —LUKE 8:26–27

How would you like it if the first person who greeted you in a strange city was a dangerous lunatic? That's exactly who met Jesus and his disciples when they crossed the Sea of Galilee and stepped out on shore. The local people had tried to bind the man in chains, but with demonic strength he would merely break the shackles and escape to roam among the tombs. The picture the Gospel paints is worse than anything out of an old Bela Lugosi film.

Confronted by such a person, most of us would have rushed back to the boat and shoved off as quickly as possible. But Jesus had crossed Galilee in a storm, precisely to heal this man, and he would not turn back. We are frightened and repulsed. Jesus is touched with compassion for a soul in torment.

Instead of rushing upon them in a fury, the demonized man falls down at Jesus' feet and shouts at the top of his voice, "What do you have to do with me, Jesus, Son of the Most High God? I beg you, do not torment me." The demons were speaking, not the man. The greater power and authority of Jesus forced them to fall at his feet, imploring his mercy. But Jesus had mercy on the man, not on the demons. He commanded them to come out and the man was restored to his right mind.

As modern men and women, we sometimes have difficulty with such stories. Didn't these people mistake mental illness with demonic possession? Such mistakes were undoubtedly made in ancient Israel, but Jesus knew precisely what he was dealing with.

Jesus was not afraid of the powers of darkness that inhabited this man. He knew his own power was far greater. And so he used it to lovingly restore him. Jesus' desire to heal our afflictions, whether emotionally, physically, or spiritually based is the same today.

God's ultimate hope for every one of us is that we will enjoy an intimate and loving relationship with him. Our communion with him is characterized by love, freedom, joy, and respect. The fallen angels, on the other hand, seek an unholy and counterfeit communion, one characterized by hatred, domination, enslavement, and terror. Quite often, evil is merely a counterfeit of the good.

We are naive if we fail to believe that powerful forces of evil are at work in the world today. But we make an even greater mistake if we fail to understand that God's power is far greater than Satan's. Two thousand years ago, Jesus commanded the unclean spirits to leave. He does the same today.

Jesus, if I am to know fear in my life, may it be the fear of God that rules me. Never let me fall into the hands of my enemy, but keep me safe within your powerful and protective arms. Don't let me be frightened or repulsed by the suffering of others, but touch my heart with compassion so that I might, in turn, touch others with your love.

New Age Angels

For Satan himself masquerades as an angel of light.
—2 CORINTHIANS 11:14

I grew up in an era that was embarrassed by religion. Personal religious beliefs were never a subject of polite conversation. Whatever could not be seen or touched simply did not really exist. To suggest otherwise marked you as either a fool or a charlatan.

Ironically, this sophisticated skepticism has actually increased our susceptibility to all kinds of primitive beliefs and superstitions. Like a beach ball pushed under water only to pop up a few feet away, our spiritual nature and spiritual longings eventually reassert themselves, sometimes in strange ways. Not surprisingly, our culture is now awash with every variety of superstition, including belief in ghosts, witches, reincarnation, spirit guides, and shamanism.

Spiritual hunger is good in one sense but dangerous in another. It is like setting someone loose in a supermarket when they haven't eaten for three days. They may bring home every kind of food imaginable, some of which begins to smell bad and taste worse after a few days on the shelf.

This new appetite is evident in the rise of the New Age movement, where a smorgasbord of spirituality is presented from which devotees can choose what they like and discard what they don't. Currently, angels are all the rage. Sophy Burnham's *Book of*

Angels, Alma Daniel's *Ask Your Angels*, and others like them have created increased interest in all kinds of spiritual beings. The problem with some of these books is that they indiscriminately draw from Christian and non-Christian sources and often fail to distinguish whether these are good or evil beings. As Peter Lamborn Wilson says, "The current New Age craze for Angels, seems to exalt a sort of greeting-card version of the Angel—warm, supportive, creative." Sometimes such books can be the first step in a spiritual search that ultimately leads to Christ. But often they are detours that lead people into the heart of darkness.

In spiritual matters, we need wise guides. We need to cultivate discernment so that we can tell what is from God and what is not. If we are seeking spiritual thrills or power rather than the truth, we can endanger our souls by dabbling in the supernatural. Scripture calls Satan the "father of lies." He's the slickest con man of all time, and one of his favorite ploys is to dress up as an angel of light, a kind of "greeting-card angel," if you will. If you fall for the disguise and open yourself to such a being, you may never know what hit you.

Author Geddes MacGregor reinforces this point when he says, "The most terrible of the afflictions that attend him who loses purity of heart is that he loses with it the power to detect evil intent when it approaches him as a wolf attired in the benign clothing of a sheep. He is an easy prey: a sitting duck for the devil. He has lost the clarity of moral vision that penetrates every disguise and sees through to the spiritual reality behind it."

As Christians, we are guided by the Holy Spirit and by God's word in the Bible. No matter how dazzling the vision, we must test the spirits against the Word of God and not allow our spiritual hungers to confuse our judgment. If we do, we will be able to spot a fake whenever we see it. Far from being a sitting duck for the devil, we will have the wisdom to discern the spirits, no matter how ingeniously disguised.

Lord, I know that you will keep me on the right path if it's really you I'm seeking. Help me not to search for the sensational, but to seek true holiness. You know that the search is neither glamorous nor easy. You said yourself that the road was narrow and hard. Help me, Lord, to follow you along that road and not to veer onto other paths, no matter how attractive they may seem.

Tempted in Eden

Now the serpent was more crafty than any of the wild animals the LORD God had made. He said to the woman, "Did God really say, 'You must not eat from any tree in the garden'?"

—GENESIS 3:1

Adam and Eve had it made. They had each other. They lived in Paradise. And they enjoyed perfect intimacy with their Creator. Then they spoiled everything. They listened to the voice of the Tempter, who placed a seed of doubt in Eve's mind.

We all know the old story. Today we suffer the painful consequences. When my niece, Jenny, was only five years old, she said something that startled me. We were driving along a city street in the middle of winter when we passed a graveyard. Jenny knew that cemeteries were filled with the bones of dead people. She turned to me and sighed, "I wish Adam and Eve had never sinned." Her little face was so sad, her voice so full of sorrow that it nearly broke my heart. Despite her tender years, she had already experienced enough pain to comprehend the dilemma of our race.

Genesis says that Adam and Eve tried to hide from God when he called their names in the garden. They knew something was terribly wrong. In fact, sin had ripped a hole in their hearts large enough to swallow the universe. No longer would they converse with God in the garden in the cool of the day. No longer would they enjoy one another's company without accusation forming a barrier between them. No longer would they even understand their own motivations. They had become alienated from God, from each other, and from themselves. All was agony, loss, and endless confusion.

God expelled them from the garden of his presence but then promised them a savior. Unlike the angels, human beings would be granted another chance. Somewhere in the long centuries ahead, a child would be born who would crush the head of the serpent. Jesus is the one who fulfills the promise. He is a beacon in the dark night of sin. He is the sinless one who by his obedience reverses our disobedience. Because Jesus obeyed his Father to the end, you and I have another chance. Because of him we have the power to prefer God's will to ours. We have the grace to believe that God is telling the truth after all. What can we say to such mercy? We can reply most eloquently with our obedience. It is the best gift of love we could ever give the Father.

In Adam and Eve the world made a bad beginning. But in Christ, the world begins anew. He is the firstborn of the new creation and we are the ones who follow in his steps.

Father, please forgive my foolishness. So many times I have preferred my version of what is good for me to yours. Sometimes I have even considered your laws arbitrary and unnecessary. I, too, have been deceived by the serpent. Let love for you compel me as it did Jesus. Never let me be mastered by the glamour of evil, but purify my heart so that I might one day be restored to Paradise.

Eight

Angels and the Unseen War

*The wars among nations on earth are merely
popgun affairs compared to the fierceness of battle
in the spiritual unseen world.*
—BILLY GRAHAM

*M*ichael the Archangel is depicted in Scripture as a great warrior, leading the host of heaven against all the demons of hell. He is also thought to be the guardian protector of God's people. It is comforting to know that powerful angels like Michael are engaged in the battle alongside us.

Though the fight is real, sometimes we wage it in anything but a wise manner. Young Christians particularly can become so excited about talk of weapons and warfare that they think spiritual combat involves shouting commands against the enemy and singing warlike songs. The truth is that spiritual warfare is only one part of the Christian life and not a very glamorous part at that. If we insist on waging it in the flesh, we will have nothing but spiritual bruises to show for it.

We need to realize that God allows us to engage in the battle in order to strengthen us. As we resist the enticements of evil, we grow in maturity. The longer we live in obedience to Christ, the greater will be our ability to destroy the strongholds of the enemy. Our weapons will impress no one, but they will be effective enough to win the war: holiness, faith, meekness, long-suffering, truth, and the knowledge of God's Word.

We do need zeal for the struggle, but let's make certain it's a godly zeal, rather than some fleshly version that will only get us into trouble. Most of all, let's remember that it's Christ who leads us into battle and who keeps us safe. Without him, we wouldn't have a chance. With him, we have the victory.

When the Devil Lives Next Door

And there was war in heaven. Michael and his angels fought against the dragon, and the dragon and his angels fought back. But he was not strong enough, and they lost their place in heaven. The great dragon was hurled down—that ancient serpent called the devil, or Satan, who leads the whole world astray. He was hurled to the earth, and his angels with him.

—Revelation 12:7–9

Like it or not, real estate values suffer whenever "undesirable elements" move into a neighborhood. Imagine how the real estate we call "earth" suffered when Satan got kicked out of heaven and thrown down to earth. I don't know about you, but I have been tempted to utter a sarcastic "thanks a lot" to Michael and his angels for ejecting Satan and his cohorts from the heavenly realms. Couldn't they have tossed him into an unpopulated region of the universe? In a sense, the devil is now everyone's neighbor. And he is definitely spoiling the neighborhood.

At least we can be thankful that Scripture warns us that the war that began in heaven now rages on earth, sometimes in our own backyard. In fact, the Book of Revelation says that the Evil One makes war on "those who keep the commandments of God and hold the testimony of Jesus." After all, it's better to know you're in a war and to arm yourself accordingly rather than to wander around, innocently stepping on land mines.

But let's get back to the neighborhood. What would you do if criminals started moving in? You could sell your house, but what if criminal elements have moved in everywhere? If even the best neighborhoods had a crook on every corner? You would simply be trading one bad neighborhood for another.

The best thing you could do in such a situation would be to arm and equip yourself. You would, no doubt, install greater security measures in your home, and you might even purchase weapons and take a course in self-defense. You would also appeal to the authorities for help.

Knowing that the devil is on the loose is a sobering matter. But the Scriptures tell us how to engage in spiritual combat so that we needn't be afraid of Satan, "for he that is in me is greater than he that is in the world." We need to arm ourselves with the tactics and weapons of heaven, rather than the strategies of this world. The more the Gospel penetrates our lives, the more we will perceive that the weapons of Christ are humility, obedience to the Father, trust and faith, truth, right living, and the Word of God, which is the "sword of the Spirit." As we appeal to God's authority for dealing with the attacks of our enemy, we will grow in confidence that Christ has given his followers authority over the Evil One.

We are not to let the neighborhood go to the devil, but we are to claim this earth for God's kingdom. As Scripture says, "The earth is the Lord's and the fullness thereof." Jesus is in the business of recapturing territory for God, and we are enlisted in his army. That's why Satan so frequently takes aim at Christians. As we fight the enemy, let us remember the prayer that Jesus taught us: "Our Father, who art in heaven, hallowed be thy name. Thy kingdom come, thy will be done, on earth as it is in heaven." Let's bring the kingdom into our own neighborhoods. The more that heaven encroaches upon the earth, the less our enemy will like it here.

Father, help me not to be naive about the spiritual conflict that rages about me. Worse yet, don't let me try to stand in my own strength. Instead, clothe me with integrity, with faith in you, with obedience to your commandments, with the knowledge of what your Son has done for me, and with the tremendous power of your Word. That way I shall be strong in the strength of your power.

The Prince of This World

You were dead through the trespasses and sins in which you once lived, following the course of this world, following the ruler of the power of the air, the spirit that is now at work among those who are disobedient.

—EPHESIANS 2:1–2 NRSV

J. R. R. Tolkien wrote an enormously popular fantasy trilogy entitled *The Lord of the Rings*. The main character, Frodo Baggins, possessed a ring of great power. Among other things, the ring had the power to render its wearer invisible to most eyes. Frodo's perilous quest involved traveling to Mount Doom in the land of Mordor in order to consign the ring to the flames of the mountain, thus destroying its terrible power forever.

Frodo and his companions were pursued by black riders, who sought to murder them and take the ring. In one encounter, Frodo panicked and slipped the ring on his finger in the hopes that it would hide him from his pursuers. What he failed to realize was that the ring actually made him visible to the evil riders and invisible to his companions. He was nearly killed in the ensuing fray. Each time Frodo succumbed to temptation by wearing the ring, he became more vulnerable to its powerful enchantments.

Disobedience works much like Frodo's ring. In our hearts, we know what God requires of us. But our pride, our fears, and our desires, tempt us to obey our will rather than God's. We prefer our definition of what is good for us to God's definition.

In his letter to the Ephesians, Paul makes it clear that whoever lives a life of disobedience to God has the ruler of the power of the air, or Satan, at work in them. The prince of this world actually feeds on our disobedience. Living a life of disobedience is like putting Frodo's ring on your finger. It makes you vulnerable to all kinds of evil. A habit of disobedience puts you firmly in the power of Satan.

Loving God, on the other hand, involves much more than simply paying lip service to him. It requires a total surrender of your life into the hands of God, obeying his commands whether or not you feel like it. As you grow in a life of obedience, your power to resist evil will increase. Much like aerobic exercise that increases lung capacity, preferring God's will to your own can increase your spiritual stamina. Rather than having the prince of this world at work in your life, you will have the power of Jesus at work within. You will be stronger and more joyful, better able to resist the enticements of the evil angels, no matter how appealing they may seem.

Jesus, you once said that your food was to do the will of your Father in heaven. I pray that this will be my food also. Nourish me by the power of your Holy Spirit that I may form a habit of obedience that will delight your angels and put my enemy to flight.

The Bread of Angels

But he himself [Elijah] went a day's journey into the wilderness. . . . He asked that he might die: "It is enough; now, O LORD, take away my life." . . . Suddenly an angel touched him and said to him, "Get up and eat." . . . He got up, and ate and drank; then he went in the strength of that food forty days and forty nights to Horeb the mount of God.

—1 KINGS 19:4–5, 8 NRSV

Elijah was an Old Testament prophet who spoke the word of the Lord in an age of idolatry. He had just enjoyed a spectacular victory over false prophets, who were destroyed after Elijah called down fire from heaven. Now we see him on the run, afraid of the evil Queen Jezebel, whose prophets he had slain. Elijah was so fearful and depressed that he asked God to take his life. But God had a better idea.

Instead, he sent an angel to touch him and nourish him in the wilderness. The food the angel brought was enough to keep Elijah going for the next forty days and nights. That's what you call high-energy snacking!

Not many of us will ever find ourselves on the lam, fleeing an evil queen. Neither are we likely to call down fire from heaven. But each of us is called to witness to the living God, and sometimes our witness will not be appreciated. Whenever we work against the idols of the age—against the lust for money, power, and sex—we will encounter great spiritual opposition.

Notice that Elijah should have been elated rather than depressed. He has just won the greatest spiritual victory of his lifetime. God had shown his power in a very dramatic way. Yet he is afraid and dejected. The tremendous faith he displayed when surrounded by the false prophets had given way to exhaustion and doubt. So much so that he does not want to go on living.

Elijah's experience is sometimes our own. We may have seen God work through us or through our prayers in a powerful new way. And yet we experience fear and dejection when we face an apparent setback. If so, we may be the target, as Elijah was, of a spiritual counterattack. We have just encroached on enemy territory, and he is not happy.

Yet God did not leave Elijah to deal with his depression on his own. Instead, he sent one of his faithful angels to touch his servant and feed him the bread of heaven. You may recall that Jesus once told his disciples that he had food to eat that they did not know about. His food was to do the will of his Father in heaven. As we seek to do God's will, to be his witnesses to an unbelieving world, we too will be nourished by the bread of angels, and our exhaustion and depression will give way to faith and hope in the incredible provision of our God.

Father, sometimes I get so tired of the fight that I wonder if it's really worth it. I even start to wonder if I've gained any ground at all. At such times, help me to see the true state of things. Don't let my enemy discourage me with lies about his power. Instead, feed me with the bread of angels and give me joy in the midst of the battle.

Fighting on the Side of the Angels

> *Our struggle is not against flesh and blood, but against the*
> *rulers, against the authorities, against the powers of this dark*
> *world and against the spiritual forces of evil in the heavenly*
> *realms.* —EPHESIANS 6:12

*P*aul is not committing the sin of hyperbole when he says
that our struggles are against the cosmic powers of darkness. The Bible is nothing if not a record of the conflict between
good and evil.

But we are so easily fooled into thinking that mere human
beings are our primary enemies. On the religious front, Christians
scandalize the world by squabbling and name-calling among
themselves. Catholics and Protestants view each other with pre-
dictable suspicion. Traditionalists accuse charismatics of charis-
mania. And purists take potshots at anyone who doesn't measure
up to their version of Christianity. Of course it's important to fight
for the solid meat of the Gospel, for the truths of our faith. But we
are often divided on the peripherals, matters that are not central
to what C. S. Lewis calls "mere Christianity." No denomination or
group is innocent in this regard. You name it, and we can find
something to fight about. In the meantime, men and women per-
ish for failure to hear the Gospel.

This same kind of contentiousness often characterizes our
dealings on the political front. We fall victim to what has been

called the political illusion: we begin to believe that every problem we face has a political solution. This adds a new intensity to the political arena, where we come just short of calling our opponent the antichrist. The truth is, we sometimes conduct ourselves in the political realm as anything but men and women whose conduct is shaped by the kindness of Christ.

True, religious and political differences can be tremendously important. But sometimes, the Evil One throws them in our faces as a smoke screen, obscuring what is really going on. For instance, we may be ruled by corrupt politicians and judges because we are simply getting what we have asked for as a nation. God may be allowing us to experience the fruit of our rebellion against him. Repentance may change things in a way that political campaigning cannot. We must develop both a spiritual and a political outlook. If we don't look below the surface to see what is going on spiritually, we will often miss the point.

Scripture tells us we are in a battle, but how sad if we mistake the real enemy and begin to fight each other instead. Our enemies are not mere flesh and blood. We fight spiritual powers, and we must fight them with spiritual weapons. While Satan and his angels employ the weapons of hatred—deceit, slander, fear, greed, and confusion—we are called to employ the weapons of love—forgiveness, mercy, faith, truth, discernment, prayer, sacrifice, and righteousness. The battle is real. We cannot ignore it. But neither can we enter the fray with delusions about who the enemy is and how we are to fight. If we want to fight on the side of the angels, we need to heed Paul's warning.

Father, help me to be wise as a serpent and innocent as a dove. Help me to know who my real enemy is and how I am to fight.

Confirm me in self-control so that I won't give in to the temptation to use dirty tricks and name-calling in the cause of "righteousness." Let me instead use the weapons of prayer, perseverance, patience, truth, obedience, and love.

Angels Protect Us from Evil

As Pharaoh drew near, the Israelites looked back, and there were the Egyptians advancing on them. . . . The angel of God who was going before the Israelite army moved and went behind them; and the pillar of cloud moved from in front of them and took its place behind them. It came between the army of Egypt and the army of Israel. And so the cloud was there with the darkness, and it lit up the night; one did not come near the other all night. —EXODUS 14:10, 19–20 NRSV

*I*f you grew up in the 1950s or '60s, you probably can't help but picture the Israelite march to the Red Sea like this: a long-haired Charlton Heston with staff in hand extended over the water, while an evil-looking Yul Brynner thunders on in hot pursuit. The Red Sea, we later discovered, was made of Jello. Thank you, Cecil B. DeMille! But the real Exodus had far more impressive special effects.

The Israelites escaped enslavement by marvelous acts of God—horrific plagues rained from heaven upon their Egyptian oppressors. But Pharaoh's hard heart could not stand the thought of Moses leading the Jewish people to freedom. So he pursued them in the desert, threatening to overtake them as they approached the Red Sea. It would be so easy for him. His powerful army would swiftly crush the raggedy band of slaves. But Pharaoh, stubborn and stupid in his wickedness, forgot about the angels.

The angel and the pillar of cloud, a symbol of God's presence, moved from the front of the people to take up protective positions behind them. As we know, Pharaoh was not able to catch the Israelites, who passed through the waters in safety. Still he stubbornly pursued them, but the walls of water engulfed him and his army, suffocating them in its turbulent wake.

The story of Exodus is played out in miniature in the life of every believer. Like the Jews of old, we are held in bondage. Pharaoh represents Satan, who enslaves every person who does not belong to God. But God saves us from our enemy and leads us into freedom and into the promised land of his presence.

While we live on earth, we are involved in this exodus journey. Often, our pilgrimage seems agonizingly slow and confusing. We seem to wander in a desert of our own weakness and sin. Our faith is tested by difficulty. We have fears, many of which are real. It is not only "the things that go bump in the night" that terrify us. We sense an evil presence intent on overtaking us.

But like the Jewish people fleeing the wrath of Pharaoh, we can be certain that God will surround us with his protection. He will send angels to battle our enemy and a pillar of fire to brighten our darkness. Though evil may threaten us, it will never overwhelm us. We can take comfort from the prayer attributed to Patrick of Ireland: "Christ be with me, Christ before me, Christ be after me, Christ within me, Christ beneath me, Christ above me, Christ at my right hand, Christ at my left." Surrounded by Christ, we will pass safely through this world to the next.

Lord, you know the spiritual dangers I have already passed through. It was your hand that kept me safe over and over again. Help me to fear neither the desert nor the darkness, but to take each step knowing that I am closer to the day when I will see you face to face, when I will live in your presence forever.

Nine

❧

When No Delivering Angel Comes

No wound? No scar?
Yet, as the Master shall the servant be,
And pierced are the feet that follow Me;
But thine are whole; can he have followed far
Who has no wound or scar?
                    —AMY CARMICHAEL

*R*are is the person who has not suffered some tragedy in life. We all know women who have been raped, men who have died of horrible diseases, children who have been abused, soldiers who have been mutilated in war. Why don't the angels come to straighten things out? Surely they have the power. Where are they when we really need them?

Anyone who believes that angels exist will certainly pose this question. Of course it is really just another form of the age-old question about good and evil. How could a good God allow evil to exist?

The answer is not simple. Part of it lies in the nature of love itself. We learn from Scripture that God is love. When he created us, he took all the risks that love demands. By this I mean that he fashioned us as beings who would be capable of either embracing or rejecting his love. Robots cannot love, but men and women can. By the same token, they can also hate. This was the tremendous risk God took in creating us as beings capable of either embracing or rejecting his love.

Evil is merely the refusal to love God. Each person makes that choice here on earth. Whenever and wherever God is spurned, evil fills our cities, our streets, and our homes. Even so, God can turn such evil on its head, compelling it to serve his purposes.

Ultimately, that is what we see in the life, death, and resurrection of Jesus of Nazareth. We see the deeper love of God triumphing despite the evil intentions of fallen angels and human beings. As we confront evil in our own lives and in the lives of those we love, we must remember that God is for us and that he will never abandon or forsake us. Ultimately, his love is a power that conquers every evil and vanquishes every foe.

How to Fight the Dark Angels

Then Jesus was led by the Spirit into the desert to be tempted by the devil. After fasting forty days and forty nights, he was hungry. The tempter came to him. . . . Then the devil left him, and angels came and attended him.

—MATTHEW 4:1–3, 11

After Jesus' baptism in the Jordan River, the Spirit led him into the wilderness to be tempted by the devil. Jesus fasted for forty days and nights in the barren wilderness and then the devil arrived to tempt him three times.

Isn't it interesting that Jesus deliberately weakened himself before engaging in combat with his archenemy, Satan? He fasted forty days and nights, and he was starving. In a sense, you could say that he made his body weak to make his spirit strong. So often the methods of heaven contradict our most basic instincts.

Notice too that the Spirit actually led Jesus into the wilderness. Jesus didn't decide on his own that it was time to take on the devil, but he allowed the Holy Spirit to initiate a season in his life in which he would endure testing and temptation. Moreover, the angels didn't appear on the scene until Jesus had successfully resisted every trick Satan threw at him. Only then did the heavenly host come and wait on him, much like a prize-fighter's attendants after a fight.

At times, the Spirit will also lead us into the wilderness to endure a time of trial. It may be a wilderness of loneliness, illness, misunderstanding, poverty, failure, or doubt. Whatever the case, we can take courage from this crucial episode in Jesus' life. For Jesus' wilderness experience actually prepared him for his public ministry. The miracles, the preaching, the healings would all characterize the most tremendous ministry the world had ever seen. But not before Jesus engaged in a fierce and terrible spiritual combat.

If you find yourself in the wilderness, perhaps you should be encouraged. God may be preparing you for a time of greater fruitfulness and joy. Such times often do not emerge without a struggle. That struggle may involve facing your own sinfulness and lack of faith. Your enemy wants to convince you that God has abandoned you and that you are good for nothing. You may long for angels to whisper "courage" in your ears, but none come. In this kind of desert, remember to cling to God. Just as Jesus prayed and fasted, keeping in vital communion with his Father, make sure that you are holding fast to God in the midst of your wilderness experience. You can't possibly face evil on your own and win. But with patience and faith you can emerge stronger and more hopeful than before.

At times you will be tempted to escape the wilderness. If you're lonely, you might find yourself rationalizing an unhealthy relationship. If you're anxious about the future, you might become obsessed with finding ways to protect yourself and your family from financial hardship. If you haven't been able to bear children, you might be tempted to try medical treatments you believe to be unethical in order to conceive. Whatever your temptations, resist the enemy and ask God for the strength to go on.

There will be an end to your wilderness, a time when the angels will come and wait upon you as they did upon Jesus. That will be a time of rejoicing, a time of moving once again in power and confidence, a time of blessing as God continues to fulfill his purpose for your life.

> *Help me, God. I am so tired of this wilderness. Sometimes I think it will never end. I feel so needy that I don't like what I see in the mirror. Are you really testing me? If so, what am I supposed to be learning? Help me to cling to you, Lord, and strengthen me against the temptations of self-pity and fear. Lead me to a place of safety.*

A Dream or a Nightmare?

Joseph had a dream, and when he told it to his brothers, they hated him all the more. —GENESIS 37:5

Aside from Cain and Abel, the story of Joseph and his brothers is one of the most famous cases of sibling rivalry ever told. The favorite of his father, Jacob, Joseph made the mistake of telling his brothers a dream he had, which seemed to imply that he would one day rule over them. In their envy, they plotted and schemed and eventually sold their younger brother as a slave to a caravan of merchants bound for Egypt.

Joseph had many years to wonder why his dream had turned into a nightmare. Hadn't God promised he would one day be great? Then why was he a slave in Egypt? Had he simply suffered from youthful grandiosity? Who was he to think that God had chosen him for some special purpose?

Yet God's promise had not changed. And Joseph turned out to be not only a dreamer but an interpreter of dreams. Called upon to analyze one of Pharaoh's dreams, Joseph predicted seven years of prosperity followed by seven years of widespread famine. Events unfolded just as Joseph predicted. Because of Joseph, Egypt was able to use the seven good years to prepare for the seven hard years. Pharaoh was so impressed by the young Hebrew slave that he made him governor of Egypt.

The famine Joseph had foreseen stretched even to Canaan, where Jacob still lived with Joseph's brothers. To fend off starvation, several of the brothers traveled to Egypt to buy grain, little knowing that their younger brother was now a man of power in the land. Through a series of surprising events, Jacob and his sons eventually moved to Egypt. In a poignant scene at the end of the Book of Genesis we see the brothers weeping as they beg Joseph's forgiveness. With incredible mercy, Joseph replies, "Even though you intended to do harm to me, God intended it for good, in order to preserve a numerous people, as he is doing today." At the right moment, God had brought Jacob and his family to a place of safety, where they could survive the years of famine.

God did not send an angel to rescue Joseph, but he gave him a magnificent dream to sustain him through the difficult years.

Perhaps he has given you a dream or made a promise to you, which now seems impossible to fulfill. Like Joseph, you may have been sinned against by someone close to you, a family member who abused you, a husband or wife who betrayed you, a person who spread lies about you. You may suffer emotional and physical scars from the sins of others. Perhaps the wounds are so deep that you feel as though you have been sold into a kind of emotional slavery, unable to break free from the hurts of the past. You may wonder why God allowed such evils to befall you. Couldn't he have spared an angel or two to protect you when you couldn't protect yourself?

If you feel this way, you may find comfort in Joseph's story. Through the long years of his bondage, Joseph did not lose faith in God. Though no angel shielded him from his brothers' evil intentions, he still clung to God. He must have suffered tremendous loneliness, rejection, depression, and confusion in the years before God fulfilled the dream. But the sins of Joseph's brothers could not thwart God's plan. Instead, he used those very sins to accomplish his purpose. The evil that Joseph suffered became the very thing God used to shape him into the kind of man capable of ruling. With infinite creativity, God once again transformed the malevolent intentions of others to fulfill his own plan.

If you have lived for any length of years, you will have suffered from the sins of someone close to you. Ask God for the grace to trust him even in the midst of your suffering. If you do, he will not let any of your anguish go to waste. Instead, he will raise you up and use you for his purposes, making something beautiful out of every tear you shed.

Father, you know the ways I have been hurt, especially when I was too young to defend myself. Please help me to let go of my bitterness and let you make something good of what I have suffered. Help me especially to forgive those who have sinned against me. Your Son suffered unjustly on the cross and now he wears his wounds as a badge of honor. Transform my wounds into something beautiful for your kingdom.

An Angel of Courage

Jesus went out as usual to the Mount of Olives, and his disciples followed him. On reaching the place, he said to them, "Pray that you will not fall into temptation." He withdrew about a stone's throw beyond them, knelt down and prayed, "Father, if you are willing, take this cup from me; yet not my will, but yours be done." An angel from heaven appeared to him and strengthened him. —LUKE: 22:39–43

*S*ometimes we make the mistake of thinking it was easy for Jesus to die for us. After all, he was God, wasn't he? He could do anything he wanted. Yet the Gospel tells us that Jesus was filled with agony and fear on the evening before his death. So much so that he asked his Father to change his mind about the Crucifixion—to save him from the "cup of suffering" he was destined to drink.

It grieves me to imagine what Jesus must have endured for my sake. Yet it also comforts me. He felt the same fear that prowls inside my soul whenever awful possibilities lurk. Like Jesus, I can honestly cry out to God and ask him to rescue me. And like Jesus, I can tell the Father that whatever happens, I want his will to be done.

The Father answered his Son, not with the response Jesus hoped for but with the answer he was willing to receive. Instead of a delivering angel, God sent an angel to impart greater courage for the terrible ordeal ahead.

For his part, Jesus urged the disciples to pray they would not fall into temptation. Despite his urging, they couldn't stay awake long enough to pray with him in that dark hour. They had just eaten the heavy Passover meal and drunk the Passover wine. How could Jesus expect them to stay awake and pray? What kind of temptation was Jesus talking about anyway?

Jesus knew that fear would rule his disciples for a time. After his arrest, Satan would appear to be ascendant. Peter, James, John, and the rest of the lot would lose faith, betray him, and run and hide. None of them would stand when the soldiers came to seize him.

We wonder how the disciples could have been such cowards. Yet we succumb to the same temptations they did. Like Peter, we tell Jesus that we love him and that we are willing to follow him anywhere. Yet we are unwilling to follow him into the darkness of fear and confusion and suffering, unwilling to believe that God will send his angels to give us courage to face the most terrible circumstances. Our faith trembles when disaster looms. We want to withdraw, to run and hide, to find a place of ultimate safety.

At such times, we need to echo Jesus' prayer. "I'm afraid, Lord. Please take this suffering from me. Even so, Father, don't answer my prayer if it contradicts your will." As we pray, God will answer us. Whether or not he spares us from the suffering we most fear, he will give us courage to face whatever comes.

Lord, you test me and often find me wanting. Sometimes I am shocked by the cowardice you uncover in me. But just as the angel strengthened you on the Mount of Olives, give me the strength to stand firm no matter what the Father asks.

Calling All Angels

"Do you think I cannot call on my Father, and he will at once put at my disposal more than twelve legions of angels? But how then would the Scriptures be fulfilled that say it must happen in this way?" —MATTHEW 26:53–54

*P*icture the scene. It is the eve of the Crucifixion. Jesus has just been seized in the Garden of Gethsemane by the soldiers of the chief priests and elders. Peter, always the leader among the disciples and a man of action, strikes the slave of the high priest, cutting off his ear. He is willing to defend Jesus to the death if need be. And then Jesus rebukes him.

A deeper logic is at work, a divine plan that throws Peter and the disciples into confusion. A battle to the death they can understand, but surrender in the face of such manifest evil? Never! And so they flee.

Reading about Peter always comforts me. He meant well, but he often made a mess of things, sometimes embarrassingly so. Yet Jesus loved him and confided in him. If it had been up to me in that dark confrontation in Gethsemane, I would have screamed loud and clear for as many legions of angels as the Father could spare. My top priority would have been to get everyone out of there alive, especially Jesus and me. I would have been like Peter, taking things into my own hands in order to avert disaster and insure that the Messiah would eventually be crowned the king of Israel.

Yet Jesus, who never acts predictably, rebuked Peter. He knew that fear, rather than the fury of the high priests and their soldiers, was his real enemy. Jesus could have summoned an angel cavalry to the rescue, but that would have meant undermining his Father's plan. True, there would have been no agonizing crucifixion, but neither would there have been a glorious resurrection. You and I would still be alienated from God and enslaved by our enemy. Jesus refrained from calling upon the power of the angels so that a deeper power could be at work, a power of obedience, of love, and of lamb-like acceptance of the plan and purpose of God.

Jesus' response still puzzles us. Like Peter, we unwittingly prefer our plan to God's. Even when we honestly want to do God's will, we often prefer to do it our way.

It's just as well that God is the only one who has the power to order the angels around. He knows when and where they can do the most good. He also knows that our salvation comes from trust and confidence in him and in his Son, not in the feeling of safety and security that we often mistake for salvation.

Father, as the heavens are higher than the earth, so are your ways higher than my ways and your thoughts higher than mine. I confess that I am so often puzzled by the way you do things, the prayers you agree with and the ones you don't. But you are the Lord. Don't let me cling to my ways over yours. Help me to let go and trust you.

Feeling Abandoned by God

"My God, my God, why have you forsaken me?"
—MATTHEW 27:46

*T*he anguished cry of Jesus from the cross resounds across the centuries to fill our own hearts with almost unbearable grief. How is it that the Son of God, the one who breathed life into Creation, was apparently conquered by death and abandoned by his Father?

Is this love, we ask? Jesus himself assured us that no earthly father would give a stone to a son who asked for bread. Yet wasn't his heavenly Father giving Jesus precisely that—a silence so stony hard as to seem like complete abandonment? Couldn't God have broken the terrifying silence with a word of encouragement as he did when Jesus was baptized in the Jordan: "This is my beloved Son, in whom I am well pleased"? But the Father said nothing as Jesus hung naked in the midday sun.

Sometimes we too feel this seemingly heartless absence of God in our lives. Where is he when a child dies, when we lose a job, suffer the pain of divorce, or feel betrayed by a fellow believer? On a larger scale, where was God when the Jews were gassed at Auschwitz? Where is he today when thousands are slaughtered in Bosnia and hundreds of thousands in Rwanda?

If God isn't willing to take away our suffering, couldn't he at least speak comforting words to us? We desperately want God to assure us that all will be well. Why isn't a blessing released to ease our pain, to assure us that we are on the right track, that God still has a wonderful plan for our lives? Of course, God often does speak to us in such circumstances, but what about the times he doesn't?

Clearly, the cost of our redemption involved tremendous inner agony as well as excruciating physical pain. And yet Jesus, uttering this heart cry, was actually repeating the first verse of Psalm 22: "My God, my God, why have you forsaken me?" By doing so, he was calling forth the words of the entire psalm. If we stop with the first verse, we fail to plumb the depths of Christ's faith in his Father, even in the midst of his suffering.

Psalm 22 continues later, saying, "You who fear the LORD, praise him! All you offspring of Jacob glorify him; stand in awe of him all you offspring of Israel! For he did not despise or abhor the affliction of the afflicted; he did not hide his face from me, but heard when I cried to him" (vv.23–24 NRSV).

Nailed to a cross, suffering a horrible death, Jesus did not deny his feeling of abandonment. His cry was an honest one. Even so, he affirmed with utter certainty his faith in the Father's goodness and in the purpose of his plan. God's ways are often so utterly foreign to us that we sometimes feel repulsed by them. Why did a good man die so that I could go free? Part of the answer to the age-old question regarding evil in the world has to do with the evil in you and me. The remedy for our sin is so radical that it startles and sometimes shames us. Through obedience, Jesus liberated us from our sin and guilt.

In the most desperate hour of his life, no angel came to deliver him or even to offer words of comfort. Yet we know that the resurrection of Jesus displayed the deeper love and faithfulness of God.

Perhaps you are facing some kind of death in your life. It may be the death of a dream or the death of a relationship or the very real death of someone you love. Remember to pray all of Psalm 22, not just the first line, for "God hears you when you cry to him."

Father, why have you abandoned me? I cry out to you but hear nothing in response. Why do you stay so far away from me? Yet you are the One who has kept me safe from the moment of my birth. Somehow, I know that you do not despise my afflictions, but you hear me when I call to you. Because of you, I will live to tell others of your faithfulness.

Ten

༉

Angels at the Moment of Our Death

Do not rejoice over a ship that is setting out to sea,
for you cannot know what storms it may encounter. . . .
But rejoice rather over a ship that has reached port
and brings home all its passengers in peace.
—ADAPTED FROM THE TALMUD

For each of us, death is a destination we cannot avoid. It represents the ultimate challenge to our faith, the end of the world as we know it. Despite all the talk of "death with dignity," there is usually very little dignity in our experience of dying. It is a time of letting go, of weakness, of humbling, a time when we can no longer ignore the limits of our humanity.

Jesus himself wept at the death of his best friend Lazarus, this despite the fact that he would soon raise him from the dead. No matter what anybody tells you, death is no friend of ours. To make matters worse, death involves a journey we make without any other human companion. We go it alone, except, that is, for the Lord and his angels.

The Bible indicates that angels are present, conveying the souls of men and women from this world into the next. By way of example, remember that angels carried the soul of the poor man Lazarus to heaven and were also present at the tomb of Jesus. Billy Graham assures us about the role of angels when he says, "Hundreds of accounts record the heavenly escort of angels at death. When my maternal grandmother died, for instance, the room seemed to fill up with a heavenly light. She sat up in bed and almost laughingly said, 'I see Jesus. He has his arms outstretched toward me. I see Ben [her husband] and I see the angels.' "

A friend of mine told me about her mother's death from cancer. "My mother died two years ago. She actually came to the Lord during the time of her illness. The night she died, my sister was near her bed. She was astonished to see my mother surrounded by a brilliant light. She said it looked like the aurora borealis. She was sure it was the angels."

If you fear death, you can take tremendous comfort that you and those you love will not have to make the journey alone. God in his tender love will never abandon those who belong to him. He will surround you with his angels to keep you from harm and lead you safely home.

The Angel in the Tomb

So Joseph bought some linen cloth, took down the body, wrapped it in the linen, and placed it in a tomb cut out of rock. Then he rolled a stone against the entrance of the tomb. . . . As they [Mary Magdalene and Mary the mother of James and Salome] entered the tomb, they saw a young man dressed in a white robe sitting on the right side.

—MARK 15:46; 16:5

Joseph was a rich man from Arimathea and a follower of Jesus. While Jesus' body still dangled on the cross, Joseph went to Pilate to request that he be allowed to bury him. So he wrapped the body in a linen cloth and laid it tenderly in his own tomb, which had recently been hewn from the rock.

Jesus' last words from the cross were, "It is finished." Joseph supposed that it was indeed finished, as he rolled a large stone across the entrance of the tomb and returned home to grieve for his dead friend. The best hope of Israel had been laid to rest on a cold slab of stone.

How could Joseph have known that his own tomb would soon be utterly transformed by the power of God? When he heard the rumor of the angel at the tomb, he must have rushed to see for himself. Did he crush the linen cloth between his fingers, the death wrap that he had himself wound around the cold corpse of Jesus? Did he question Mary Magdalene about the angel's exact words: "Do not be alarmed; you are looking for Jesus of Nazareth, who was crucified. He has been raised; he is not there."

Every one of us can take comfort from the fact that Jesus was raised from the dead in the tomb of another man. It is as though the dead Jesus was laid to rest in our own graves. Because he trusted in the Father, he submitted to the terrible power of death. And God, through a greater power, raised him to life as the first-born of the new creation.

One day we too will know the cold chill of death. The thought of it frightens us. But we can take courage, as Joseph must have, from knowing that Jesus was laid to rest in our graves first. Just as death could not hold him in its grip, it will not be able to hold us. Like Jesus, we will be raised to a new life. And the angel will say to those at the grave, "Why do you seek the living among the dead?"

> *Father, I ask that at the hour of my death, you will comfort me with the knowledge that Jesus was laid to rest in my grave first. Just as death had no power to hold him, so it will have no power to hold me. In that moment, may I proclaim with Paul, "O death, where is your victory? O grave, where is your sting?"*

Aunt Kate and the Angels

*Even though I walk through the valley of the shadow of death,
I will fear no evil, for you are with me; your rod and your staff,
they comfort me.* —PSALM 23:4

ayne Herring is a Presbyterian pastor in Memphis, Tennessee, who knows that angels sometimes show up just when we need them most.

"My aunt, Kate Lewis, loved Christ all her life. She and my uncle had no children of their own, and my aunt treated me like her own son. On the day I announced my intention to enter the ministry, no one in my family rejoiced at the prospect, except my Aunt Kate, that is. She was thrilled and promised to pray faithfully for me. Her faith and love made such an impression that I eventually named one of my daughters after her.

"Five years ago my aunt lay dying of congestive heart failure. In her late eighties, her frail body was no match for the disease. Her struggle with death was prolonged and agonizing. She was gasping for breath and had been semi-comatose for many days. At one point the nurses actually tried to revive her by initiating some heroic measures to prolong her life. My father was at my aunt's bedside when it happened. Suddenly Aunt Kate sat straight up and looked around at everyone in the room. Her eyes were sharp and her speech clear, but she wasn't happy. 'Why on earth did you bring me back?' she scolded. 'It's been wonderful. I've been with the angels and I didn't want to leave!' These were her last words.

She sank back down on her pillow, and a few days later she was gone."

Like Kate Lewis, all of us will one day make the journey from this life to the next. Most of us are apprehensive about our deaths. What will it be like to stand on the edge of what has been called the ultimate frontier? How will we endure the emotional and physical suffering that death often entails? We wonder if, after all, there really is anything on the other side. Will we close our eyes never to open them again? Is death a massive black hole from which we will never emerge?

Aunt Kate hadn't wanted to come back even for a few moments, let alone a few days. But maybe God allowed her to return for our sakes. We need reassurance about the difficult transition from this life to the next. Most of us prefer the hard dirt of earth to the white clouds of heaven. This world may be far from perfect, but at least it's a world we know. When the time comes for our journey towards eternity, we need reassurance that we and those we love will not be left to make the trip alone. At the moment we die, God will send an escort of angels to convey our souls safely into paradise. Anyone who loves God and belongs to his Son will one day stand in his presence, enjoying his company forever. Who knows? Kate Lewis may even be standing by the gate, ready to greet us when we get there.

Lord, I admit that I am afraid to die. I've seen the face of death in hospitals and funeral homes, and it's not pretty. Because your Spirit lives in me, I know that you will give me an eternity of days to spend with you. Give me courage to make the journey when the time comes. Then send your angels to carry me swiftly to your loving arms.

Can't You See the Angels?

"The time came when the beggar died and the angels carried him to Abraham's side." —LUKE 16:22

*J*oann Kruse's cousin suffered from leukemia as a young child. "I can't remember a time when Catherine wasn't sick. I always felt so sorry for her. She could never do all the fun things other kids could.

"My Uncle Ray and Aunt Delores had both been raised in Christian homes but had left their faith behind many years earlier. They seemed very bitter about it and didn't want to have anything to do with the church. They even seemed estranged from the rest of the family. When Catherine became ill, they had such a hard time coping.

"Poor Catherine was frightened of dying and my aunt and uncle didn't know what to say to comfort her. Finally, a family friend began to talk to her about God and his angels. He told Catherine that God loved her very much, so much so that he had provided angels to watch over her. When the time came for her to make the journey to heaven, the angels would be there to keep her safe, he told her.

"I remember the year Catherine turned ten. It was the beginning of the end. She became so weak that she couldn't even sit up in bed anymore. While my aunt and uncle were keeping vigil one afternoon at her bedside, she shocked them by suddenly sitting straight up and pointing. 'Can't you see the angels? They're all around us!' she said excitedly.

"Uncle Ray asked her what the angels were doing. 'They're laughing and one of them is stretching out his arms and asking me if I would like to go with them,' the little girl replied.

"'Would you like to go?' my uncle asked.

"'If it's all right with you and Mom,' she replied. It must have broken their hearts, but both parents nodded their assent, and Catherine stretched out her small arms, reaching toward invisible hands. The very next instant, she was gone.

"Uncle Ray and Aunt Delores were never the same after that. Catherine's vision and the peace and joy that accompanied her death marked the beginning of their return to faith and their reconciliation with the rest of our family. In fact, Uncle Ray is the one who told me the story of Catherine's death. Both of them are gone now. I can't help but think how glad they must be to be back in each other's arms, surrounded by the angels who took such good care of them here on earth."

Father, you are the Author of life. You give life and you take it away. Thank you for creating each of us, for knitting us together in our mothers' wombs. Indeed, we are fearfully and wonderfully made. Before we are born, you know the story of our lives. You have numbered every one of our days before even one of them exists. Watch over us, Lord, and watch over our children. When the time comes, carry us home safely, borne on the wings of angels.

On the Side of the Angels?

They shouted, "This is the voice of a god, not of a man."
Immediately, because Herod did not give praise to God, an
angel of the Lord struck him down, and he was eaten by worms
and died. —ACTS 12: 22–23

So far, we've been telling consoling stories about angels and how they help us at the moment of death. But, it's important to realize that the good angels aren't always sweetness and light to everyone they meet.

In this case, an angel actually caused the death of a man who had for years been opposing God. King Herod Agrippa had killed James, the brother of John. He had also taken Peter prisoner, but, as we know, an angel came and freed him before Herod could do him the intended harm.

Like Herod the Great and Herod Antipas before him, Herod Agrippa did his best to oppose the spread of the gospel so that he could consolidate his own power. What Herod failed to realize was that he was opposing more than mere flesh and blood. He had taken his stand on the wrong side of the angels—an extremely dangerous place to be. The end for this wretched man came when he allowed people to worship him as God. Imagine his terror when his body was devoured by a repulsive and horrible disease.

Scripture shows the angels ministering God's judgment nearly as frequently as they carry his messages. Much as we would like to, we simply cannot tame the angels, just as we cannot tame God. They are loving to those who love God and terrible to those who oppose him.

As God's people, we can rejoice in all the works that the angels perform. What kind of God would let evil go unopposed forever? The believers in Jerusalem must have been glad that their enemy could no longer do them harm. Evil men and women who refuse to repent need to face the consequences of their deeds.

But we also must realize that God is the only one who can pronounce judgment. Until he does, our task is to continue to pray for our enemies. If we do, we will be certain to stand on the side of the angels.

> *Father, you remind us that vengeance belongs to you alone. I thank you that you are just and that you do not allow evil to go unpunished. Lord, I pray for those who seem captivated by evil, those who kill and brutalize and live only for themselves. Help them to repent so that they will know your mercy rather than your wrath.*

Are You Ready to See an Angel?

So that through death he [Jesus] might destroy the one who has the power of death, that is, the devil, and free those who all their lives were held in slavery by the fear of death. For it is clear that he did not come to help angels, but the descendants of Abraham.   —HEBREWS 2:14–15 NRSV

We hear a lot these days about near-death experiences. Some people believe they are caused by chemical reactions in the brain. Others believe they are authentic spiritual experiences. Still others suspect they are satanic deceptions foisted on the gullible. Such things are often difficult to discern, but my theory is that some of the visions are authentic while others are deceptive, and only wisdom can tell the difference.

I have another pet theory and that is that everybody is blessed with at least one Aunt Betty in their lives. I live near a small town that even has an Aunt Betty's Restaurant. Most of my friends have an Aunt Betty tucked away somewhere in their family. My own Aunt Betty was my mother's only sister. If you don't have an Aunt Betty, I'm sorry for you.

Anyway, my Aunt Betty was the kind of aunt who always showed up with huge cookies, fresh from the bakery. She was my mother's best friend and my favorite aunt. So it was heartbreaking to hear the news that cancer had spread throughout her body and that she had only a few months to live.

My aunt wasn't a particularly religious woman. She lived her life as many people do, focused on family and friends, but not especially aware of the spiritual dimension of life—or so it seemed to me. As time went on, the disease got the upper hand and my aunt had to be hospitalized. At one point, she had a vision that she later confided to her physician and to my mother. It seems she was walking in the direction of a being who was radiating light, but she was terrified to draw any closer to this being. When her doctor heard the story, he told her that there was nothing to fear. If it happened again, she should keep walking toward the light. But I wasn't so sure. Many people who claim to have had a near-death experience describe feelings of peace and joy in the presence of this "being of light." Why was my aunt so afraid? I wondered if her fear came from the fact that she wasn't yet ready to die.

As it happened, she hung on for a couple of months, and my mother and I were able to share our faith with her. My aunt prayed a prayer committing her life to the Lord shortly before she died.

My aunt's passing was anything but easy, but I pray that when she left, she was ready to see the angel of the Lord. I believe that God had mercy on her and gave her the chance to surrender her life to him before it was too late. Though she suffered greatly, her disease allowed her time to make her peace with God. When the angel of death came for the final time, I hope she met him unafraid.

Jesus, you didn't die for the angels but for us. I ask that you will pour out your grace unstintingly to those in my family who have not yet surrendered their lives to you. Spare them no suffering that will be necessary for them to come to a saving knowledge of you. Reveal yourself to them while there is yet time. Stretch out the long arms of your mercy and bring them into your kingdom.

Eleven

❧

Angels and the End of the World

We will not all sleep, but we will all be changed—
in a flash, in the twinkling of an eye, at the last trumpet.
For the trumpet will sound, the dead will be raised
imperishable, and we will be changed.
—1 CORINTHIANS 15:51–52

The world had a beginning and it will certainly have an end. Suddenly, like a "thief in the night," the final day will come upon us. The Bible predicts the end of the world, painting many frightening scenes complete with earthquakes, wars, famine, falling stars, pestilence, satanic beasts, the smoke of hell, and even the Whore of Babylon. Whatever you make of it, it's not a very pretty picture.

Despite Jesus' clear warning that nobody but the Father knows exactly when the world will end, many people persist in trying to predict just how and when it will occur. At the other extreme are those who ignore the Scripture and act as though the world as we know it will continue forever. The wise person will embrace neither extreme. Rather, each of us should heed Jesus' advice to live in readiness for the end, to strive by God's grace to be faithful lovers of God every moment of every day.

Many of the scenes regarding the end of the world come from the Book of Revelation, a complex and controversial part of the Scripture. Does it primarily address the situation of the early church or is it really talking about the end times? What is the meaning of the Beast and the Whore of Babylon? Will Christ literally establish a one-thousand year reign? To complicate matters, there are often multiple meanings of the text. Certain portions of Revelation may indeed apply both to the early church and to the end times. We cannot know for sure. However, one thing is certainly clear: each of us will one day be part of the judgment that is final, when we will stand before God who with a word will pronounce the true condition of our souls. Did we follow the Lamb or did we pledge allegiance to the Prince of this World?

When that time comes, may we be ready. If we are, it will be a day of rejoicing rather than a day of terror. At last, we will be united with the cherubim and seraphim, with Michael and Gabriel, with all the saints, and with the Savior, who is the King of Kings and Lord of Lords.

Four Angels and Four Demons

*I saw four angels standing at the four corners of the earth,
holding back the four winds of the earth. . . . I saw another
angel coming up from the east, having the seal of the living
God. He called out in a loud voice to the four angels who had
been given power to harm the land and the sea: "Do not harm
the land or the sea or the trees until we put a seal on the foreheads of the servants of our God."*

—REVELATION 7:1–3

So many incredible events have paraded across the world's
stage in recent years, from the collapse of communism to
the promise of peace in the Middle East to riots and earthquakes
in Los Angeles and devastating floods in midwestern America. We
watch them unfold moment by moment in our own living rooms,
on the modern miracle we call TV. So compelling is the coverage
and so earth-shattering the events, that I wonder if someday we
will be watching the end of the world on CNN.

John's vision must have been more vivid than anything our
high-definition screens could produce: four angels standing at the
four corners of the earth! These powerful beings were holding
back "the four winds of the earth" until God's servants were sealed
and protected from the coming devastation. As frightening and
mystifying as such scenes from the Book of Revelation are, we can
take comfort from the fact that those who belong to God will ultimately be shielded from evil in that terrible day.

But what exactly will we be protected from? Some Christians believe that they will be snatched up to heaven before calamity strikes. Others believe that God's promised protection has more to do with spiritual safety. Those who love God and live according to his Word will receive the grace to endure the most devastating circumstances and still remain faithful to Christ. They will be sealed from the demonic powers, symbolized by the four winds, that will try to destroy their relationship with God. This makes sense to me. God doesn't always protect us from physical or emotional suffering, but he does preserve the souls of those who belong to him.

Consider the case of Piedmont, Alabama. In April 1994, it was just another sleepy southern town where faith flourished. Rick Bragg of the *New York Times* described it like this: "This is a place where grandmothers hold babies on their laps under the stars and whisper in their ears that the lights in the sky are holes in the floor of heaven. This is a place where the song 'Jesus Loves Me' has rocked generations to sleep, and heaven is not a concept, but a destination.

"Yet in this place where many things, even storms, are viewed as God's will, people strong in their faith and their children have died in, of all places, a church." On Palm Sunday, a tornado ripped through Goshen United Methodist Church, killing twenty people, six of them children. The pastor's four-year-old daughter, Hannah, was among those who lost their lives.

Why would God allow such a thing to happen to people who loved him and who had gathered to worship him? We may never know the answer. Yet here's what the people of Piedmont had to say about it:

Vera Stewart, Piedmont's seventy-year-old mayor: "No matter how dark it is, if I have faith, I have a song in the night."

The pastor of Goshen United Methodist: "Having your faith shaken is not the same as losing it."

Sam Goss, who runs a local filling station: "It's hard not to question God in this. But they say there ain't no tears in heaven. We're the ones left to hurt. You see, God took them because they were ready to go. He's just giving all the rest of us a second chance."

Clearly, God doesn't spare his children from suffering, but he does spare our souls. We may or may not be living in the end times. But one thing is certain. The world will end abruptly for each of us on the day we die. Before that time, we may have to endure many earth-shattering and faith-shaking events. But as we cling to the living God, he will set an indelible seal upon our foreheads, preserving our souls so that we can spend eternity loving and being loved by him.

Father, the world I live in seems more chaotic and violent each year. Even so, I don't know whether these are the last days. You are the only one who knows the day and the hour. But I am certain that this world will end for me one day. Preserve my soul from harm and bring me safely into your kingdom. Let me live in the sacrament of the present moment, spending each hour of each day as though it is my last.

God's Second-Best Gift

Then the seven angels who had the seven trumpets prepared to sound them. The first angel sounded his trumpet, and there came hail and fire mixed with blood, and it was hurled down upon the earth. —REVELATION 8:6–7

*S*uch vivid images from the Book of Revelation both fascinate and frighten us. They seem a far cry from the jubilant notes sounded by Louie Armstrong's rendition of "When the Saints Go Marching In." Seven angels, seven trumpets, hail, fire, and blood! Whatever was going on, you can be sure that the seven angels hadn't gathered with their trumpets for a heavenly jam session.

In the ancient world, the Jews blew a trumpet to call for an assembly or to signal a battle. In this celestial scene, the angels are the trumpeters. Every time they blow their horns something terrifying happens.

Why would God's angels want to terrify us? Throughout Revelation, we see a colorful array of angelic beings moving swiftly across the universe carrying out God's commands. Scripture makes clear that they are God's servants, whose actions express his wrath to an arrogant and unbelieving world. But how could a loving God ever be full of wrath?

When the Bible talks about the "wrath of God," it does not mean that God is having some kind of celestial temper tantrum.

He never loses his temper as you and I do. Rather, "the wrath of God" is an expression that conveys the consequences of what happens whenever we choose to turn away from God. Biblical scholar George Montague puts it this way, "One cannot turn from the light without experiencing the darkness, nor from love without experiencing bitterness, nor from life without experiencing death. . . . God's wrath is not spite. It is his second-best gift to the one who has refused the first gift of his love; it is also given to bring humanity to repentance."

When the world becomes blind and deaf to God, he resorts to drastic measures. To catch our attention, the angels sound the harsh notes of the trumpet. Through them, God displays what one author has called his "severe mercy."

Often, God sounds a brash trumpet in our own lives in order to save us and call us back to himself. He does this by allowing us to experience the bitter fruits of our own bad choices. The successful young businessman who is diagnosed with AIDS. The alcoholic who loses her job and her self-respect. The pharisaical preacher who is caught in adultery and publicly mocked for his hypocrisy.

God takes no pleasure in evil. But he sometimes allows it in the hope that it will humble us and bring us to our senses. That's what these angelic trumpeters are all about—sounding the large notes of God's mercy so that human beings will admit their desperate need and be reconciled to God.

Father, help me to see the true hideousness of sin. Forgive me for tolerating it and making light of it in my life. May I detest it as much as you do. Never let me be captivated by the glamour of evil, but, instead, purify my heart. Please work in the hearts of men and women who are mesmerized by evil. Open their eyes to their peril. Show them your mercy, even if it seems severe.

Angels at the End

"The Son of Man will send out his angels, and they will weed out of his kingdom everything that causes sin and all who do evil. They will throw them into the fiery furnace, where there will be weeping and gnashing of teeth. Then the righteous will shine like the sun in the kingdom of their Father."

—MATTHEW 13: 41–42

*J*esus himself warns us that there will be hell to pay at the last judgment. His angels will separate the good from the bad, tossing the latter into a fiery furnace.

Talk of hell is no longer popular in many circles. Jesus' warning is uncongenial to modern ears. We would rather believe that the hell we make on earth will one day be swallowed up into a heaven from which no one will be excluded. But Jesus spoke about the reality of hell not to terrorize us into the kingdom as we sometimes try to do to each other. He knew that heaven would not be heaven if it were populated by evil men and women. He told us about hell because he didn't want us to be forever separated from his love. Just as it would be cowardice to look the other way when a drunken friend climbs behind the wheel of a car, it is cowardice to deny that someone's choices can drive them straight to hell.

Jesus' words remind us of the parable he told about the wheat and chaff. An enemy sowed weeds in the same plot that a farmer planted wheat. The farmer decided to let the wheat grow up alongside the weeds. At harvest time, he would pull up the weeds and throw them on the fire.

The parable is about the world we live in and about what will happen at the last judgment, when human beings will have to account for how they lived. Even so, the image of the weeds and wheat has often struck me as a vivid picture of my own divided heart. One moment I am patient, thoughtful, and understanding, and the next I am irritable, insensitive, and unkind. How can one heart include so much darkness and so much light at the same time? To echo Saint Paul, "I do not understand my own actions. For I do not do what I want, but I do the very thing I hate."

This is a troubling admission, but one that we must honestly explore. The more we know of God's mercy, the greater our courage to face the true condition of our own hearts. We can do this because God's Spirit really does live inside us. This is not just a lovely metaphor to make us feel good. As we yield ourselves to the Spirit, we will receive the grace to turn from our sins, and we will find that our hearts will produce the true wheat of his goodness. We will no longer be so divided and confused, unable to do the good things we intend. Then, when the last day finally arrives, an angel will take hold of our hands and graciously lead us into the company of the righteous and into the shining presence of the One who loves us and calls us his own.

My Father, you know how often I operate from mixed motives. I flatter people because I want to get my way. I'm nice because I'd rather do anything than face conflict. I go the extra mile because I want everybody to say how great I am. Lord, please expose the true condition of my heart to me. If you don't show me, I won't see it. If you don't give me grace to know your love in the midst of my sin, I'll be crushed by the truth. Once you show me, heal my heart and make it whole.

Angels and the Second Coming

*"When the Son of Man comes in his glory, and all the angels
with him, he will sit on his throne in heavenly glory. All the
nations will be gathered before him."*

—MATTHEW 25:31–32

At the end of the world, catastrophe will chase itself
like a dog after its tail. Just when you think that every
bit of real estate is either flooded out, burned up, or caved in,
some new disaster will hit. Yet Scripture assures us that these
frightening events merely represent the end of one world and the
beginning of the next. It is as though a heavenly contractor were
destroying block after block of ugly tenements before raising the
structures of eternity on the newly cleared land. To use a scriptural
metaphor, the end of the world will be but the birth pangs of the
new creation.

At the center of the drama is Christ himself, the long-
awaited Messiah who, this time, returns to claim his throne. No
longer will his rule be contested, his name dishonored, his ways
ignored. Every human being, from presidents to prostitutes, will
acknowledge him, either with joy or with terror. Nations will
tremble in his presence and in the presence of all his angels.

In this passage in Matthew's Gospel, Jesus tells us how to
live in a way that will ready us for history's dramatic conclusion.
"Then the King will say to those on his right, 'Come, you who are
blessed by my Father; take your inheritance, the kingdom pre-

pared for you since the creation of the world. For I was hungry and you gave me something to eat, I was thirsty and you gave me something to drink, I was a stranger and you invited me in.'"

He makes it so simple for us: if we love him and belong to him, we will take care of the sick, visit those in prison, clothe those who are naked. On the world's last day, Christ will put an end to selfishness, conceit, pride, anger, deceit, bitterness, and greed.

Right now, he offers each of us the power to put an end to these things in our own lives, to tear down the ugly tenements of sin inside our souls. As we do, we will one day thrill to the news of his coming and to the greatest invitation of all time: "Come, you who are blessed by my Father. Welcome to the heavenly kingdom, and to the inheritance which belongs to you."

Lord, help me realize that the world as I know it will not last forever. While I long for the day of your coming, establish your kingdom more completely in my own heart. Help me to befriend the lonely, to love the people I find unattractive, and to be willing to "waste" time on those who need me most. Take what little I have, Lord, and multiply it for your purposes.

Angels in Paradise

Then the angel showed me the river of the water of life, as clear as crystal, flowing from the throne of God and of the Lamb. . . .No longer will there be any curse. The throne of God and of the Lamb will be in the city, and his servants will serve him. They will see his face, and his name will be on their foreheads. There will be no more night. They will not need the light of a lamp or the light of the sun, for the Lord God will give them light. —Revelation 22:1–5

Chapters 21 and 22 in the Book of Revelation are some of the most beautiful and comforting in all of Scripture. Finally, the blood, the smoke, and the terrible destruction of this apocalyptic vision are drawing to a close. Evil has been utterly destroyed and God is wiping away every last tear from every last eye. Death and mourning and crying and pain are words now relegated to an archaic dictionary. The night is gone and darkness has vanished. This, at last, is the world we have dreamed of all our lives. A world in which love prevails and sorrow is forever banished. A world in which we never misunderstand and are never misunderstood. We have come home to a land of ecstasy, where we will see God face to face for an eternity of days.

Even with the help of Revelation, Paradise is hard to contemplate. How can we possibly imagine a world we have never even glimpsed? Perhaps we envision heaven as the cessation of our sufferings. But this is only a negative vision—the relief we feel from the absence of pain. Who among us can imagine what it will be like to be constantly encircled by joy?

Even so, I wonder if Paradise will be more familiar than we think. After all, we were made to live in it. Haven't we tasted it many times already? The rising sun infusing the morning dew with light, each drop a jewel that dangles on the soft grass. The joy of watching a newborn open his eyes in wonder at the new world. The unshakable love of husband and wife conveyed in a glance or gesture. A word of kindness when we need it most. The special taste of God at unexpected times, when he seems intent on inebriating us with his love.

It is only too easy to forget about Paradise in the world we live in. But if we open our eyes, we may yet catch a glimpse of it. Why not take a moment to reflect on these two chapters of Revelation? Let God show you the kind of eternity he has prepared for you. Remember that you were made not just for this world, but for the world that is to come.

Lord, you told us that you go before us to prepare a place for us in heaven. You even spoke of many mansions. When I am tempted to think that the sorrows of this world will never end, raise my eyes to heaven. Help me to think about whatever is true, whatever is honorable, whatever is pure, whatever is lovely, whatever is admirable, whatever is excellent or worthy of praise—whatever things will be present with you forever in Paradise.

*T*welve

ﾟ

With the Angels on Our Side

*I said to the man who stood at the gate of the year,
"Give me a light that I may tread safely into the
unknown." And he replied, "Go out into the darkness and
put your hand into the hand of God. That shall be to
you better than light and safer than a known way."*
—Minnie Louise Haskins

The angels have played a part in our past and in our present, and they will certainly play an important role in our future. We don't know the challenges we will face tomorrow morning let alone next year or the year after. But God does, and he can set his angels in motion on our behalf.

Perhaps they will come with a word of encouragement, or with an exhortation to repentance, or with a call that only we can fulfill. They may carry answers to our prayers from the very throne of God. They may show themselves to us in dreams. Whatever happens, we know that if we love Christ, we will have the angels on our side.

How can we go wrong when the angels are rooting for us? Try to remember this the next time you face some kind of unfolding disaster, the next time you make a major decision, the next time you pray for God's intervention. We may yet suffer many indignities in this life, but the truth is we are destined for a life of eternal bliss.

Meanwhile, the angels are part of God's provision to help us through the snares of this world. In the service of Christ, they can keep our souls intact and our future secure. Right now they have their work cut out for them, but one day, when we are at last home safe, the angels will breathe a sigh of relief, put their feet up, and take a well-deserved vacation, knowing that they can spend the rest of eternity savoring the memory of a job well done.

Eavesdropping on Angels

Then I looked and heard the voice of many angels.

—REVELATION 5:11

athy Deering has never seen an angel, but she's pretty sure she overheard two angels conversing in the middle of the night. "I felt I should talk to a friend about a concern I had regarding her life but was afraid of broaching the subject. Should I say something? Should I just keep quiet? Maybe I was being a busybody, but if I didn't talk to her, who would? I kept going back and forth in my mind. The more I prayed, the stronger my conviction that I should get up the nerve to tell my friend what was worrying me, so I set up a time to meet with her.

"That night a small noise woke me. I listened with my eyes closed. (I didn't bother opening them because I can't see a thing without my glasses anyway.) From the corner of my bedroom, I heard two soft voices. One said, 'Is she really going to do it?' 'Yes!' replied the other.

"Somehow, I knew that the conversation I was overhearing concerned my decision to speak with my friend. I fell asleep again and awoke with the conviction and courage I needed to be honest with her. As it turned out, she really appreciated my frankness and everything worked out really well. Later she told me that her life was changed as a result of our conversation.

"I'm convinced that the voices I heard belonged to angels. Maybe my guardian angel was actually conversing with hers. I don't really know. All I know is that their words gave me the courage I needed, the last shove over the edge, so that I was able to do what God wanted."

Kathy's story assures us that the angels are involved in our lives. They care about the decisions we make and stand by to help us. We may be uncertain about a direction we should take, a decision we should make, a difficult conversation we should initiate. If we surrender these things in prayer, we can be confident that God will help us discern the right course of action. He may give us a growing sense that one choice is better than another. He may increase our courage to take risks. He may present us with several good possibilities from which we are free to choose. Along the way, we may stumble a bit, but, with the angels on our side, we needn't worry about making any fatal mistakes.

Father, sometimes I wish I could hear you more clearly. I'm not always sure what to do. Even so, you know that I really want to live my life in a way that pleases and delights you. Sharpen my hearing, Lord, so that you won't have to shout to get my attention. Let me listen to the still, small voice that speaks to me of your love and of your will.

Put a Smile on Your Angel's Face

"I tell you, there is rejoicing in the presence of the angels of God over one sinner who repents." —LUKE 15:10

The angels get excited whenever men and women begin to face the truth about themselves. They know that ever since Adam and Eve, we have been playing hide-and-seek with God and with each other, afraid to face the darkness in our own hearts and unwilling to admit our desperate need for God's forgiveness. Because the angels love us, they want to see us reconciled to the source of all joy, to God himself. But they know this is impossible until we are honest about our true condition.

This honesty is rare and painful, little evidenced in our world. The nightly news regales us with a parade of victims and victimizers: one political party points the finger at another, hideous crimes are rationalized because the perpetrators were once victims, rivalries between public figures are celebrated in television miniseries. Surrounded by a culture in which "nobody is to blame," we find it hard to face up to the wrongs we inflict on others. Secretly, we may despise ourselves for our faults and failings, but we display a defiant face to the world.

Fortunately, God does not fall for our ruses. He presses in on us, hoping that we will turn to him and tell him we're tired of pretense, that we've had enough, that we can't seem to become the kind of people we want to be. That is what repentance is all about:

turning toward God and away from sin. As we turn to God, we will find him utterly more attractive than the evil magnetism of sin. As we humble ourselves, he will draw near.

It is true that we are both sinners and sinned against. As such, we are victims of other people's wrongdoing. Even so, we are responsible for our own sinful reactions to those who inflict harm on us. We can either choose to perpetuate the deforming power of sin by responding in kind or we can snap the cycle through forgiveness. Our future happiness depends upon the choice we make.

God treats us, after all, with tremendous dignity. He will not demean us by assenting to the lie that we are incapable of changing. He will not degrade us by stripping us of personal responsibility. True, if we insist, he will allow us to carry on the pretense that we aren't really that bad and that we can handle our lives well enough on our own.

But if we want to put a smile on an angel's face, we will stop hiding the truth about ourselves from ourselves. We will begin to realize that God already knows the worst about us and loves us anyway. We will realize that the angels themselves are rejoicing over us, the one sinner who repents.

Father, even remorse is your gift. Help me to admit the spiritual sickness that I struggle with, and then give me a soul-deep sorrow for my sin. May it be the kind of sorrow that causes me to run to you for healing, rather than the kind that makes me flee from you in fear. May my repentance be a catalyst for healing—a promise of a future filled with your mercy and loving-kindness.

A Wing and a Prayer

He [Gabriel] came and said to me, "Daniel, I have now come out to give you wisdom and understanding. At the beginning of your supplications a word went out, and I have come to declare it, for you are greatly beloved. So consider the word and understand the vision." —DANIEL 9:22–24 NRSV

The Jewish people had ignored repeated warnings to turn away from their sin or face the consequences. Obstinate in their disregard for God, these stiff-necked people were finally conquered by one of the ancient world's most powerful nations: dreadful Babylon. As a result, Daniel and many others like him were forced into captivity, exiled from their beloved Jerusalem.

But Daniel never sulked or complained about his predicament, insisting that he was being punished unfairly. Instead, he knelt before God and beseeched him to have mercy on his people. Though Daniel had not himself sinned, he stood with those who had, humbling himself and repenting of their sin. Evidently, God could not resist the prayers of such a man. The angel Gabriel actually told Daniel that a word went out from heaven because of his prayer. And whenever God speaks a word, things really do begin to happen. Incredible as it seems, we learn from this story that our prayers can actually set heaven in motion. Sometimes they even have the power to dispatch angels with a message of wisdom.

Much of the world today is engulfed in spiritual blindness, obstinate in its disregard for God. And all of us, believers and unbelievers, are suffering the consequences of this failure to live in obedience. The local news of any large city disgorges stories that horrify and depress us. Murder, child abuse, gang violence, rape—this is the standard fare we wake up to each morning. Our families are ripped apart by bitter divorces. Our children can't seem to find their way. We feel a gnawing sense of tension and anxiety as we attempt to cope with life on these terms. The truth is that our culture is dying of its sins, of its arrogance, of its failure to admit the need for God's mercy.

As Christians, we may feel it's unfair that we are consigned to such a world. After all, we may not be perfect people but at least we are trying to live in a way that honors God. But complaining merely wastes God's time and ours. We are in the midst of this mess for a reason: to share the light that lives in us, a light that is far stronger than the darkness that threatens. Like Daniel, let us fall to our knees, acknowledging our sins, begging God's mercy, and identifying with the stiff-necked people around us. As we do, we might even find we have a few kinks of our own to work out.

God can't possibly resist the prayers of a humble people. If we turn to him and beg for his mercy, he may even send out a powerful word that will set us on a new course and stop the cultural slide we have been experiencing for so many years. Daniel's prayers got Gabriel moving. Maybe the angels are standing by, ready to bring us a word in response to our prayers, a word that will impart a deeper vision and fill us with a more vivid and unshakable hope for the future.

Oh God, you have been patient with us though we have turned from your light and descended into darkness. I am not foolish enough to come before you on account of my own integrity. Instead, I come before you because of your great mercy. Oh Lord, hear; O Lord, forgive; O Lord, listen and act and have mercy on us!

When an Angel Calls Your Name

When the angel of the Lord appeared to Gideon, he said, "The Lord is with you, mighty warrior.". . . "But Lord," Gideon asked, "how can I save Israel? My clan is the weakest in Manasseh, and I am the least in my family."

—JUDGES 6:12,15

*G*ideon was a farmer and not a very successful one at that. Every time he or any other Israelite would plant a crop, their enemies, the Midianites, would swoop down upon them and destroy it. He was hardly a tough guy, and yet the angel called him a mighty warrior. Gideon responded as you or I might have: "Who, me? You must be kidding!"

But the angel kept on with his message and commissioned Gideon to save Israel from their enemies. Gideon still doubted so he asked that God give him a sign to confirm his word, and God did. Despite all odds, he fulfilled the call God had placed on his life. At one point, he led a mere three hundred men against a horde of enemies and defeated them. The angel knew what he was talking about when he called Gideon a mighty warrior.

God has created each of us for a purpose. Our primary purpose is to love and be loved by him. But he also gives us a mission to accomplish in our lifetime. We may not be called to lead an army like Gideon, but we may be asked to embark on a particular career, to raise a family, or to accomplish great things through prayer. Inevitably, we will face times in which we simply do not feel up to the task. We will not want to face one more screaming child, one more day on a stressful job, one more person who needs our prayers.

When that happens, it might be worth thinking about Gideon and the angel that called his name. Gideon knew he had none of the right credentials for saving Israel. As he pointed out to the angel, he was the low man on the totem pole. That may even have been why the angel called his name. God wanted there to be no mistake about who would deserve the credit for saving Israel. A stronger man than Gideon might have demanded the glory for himself. At one point, Gideon had rallied thirty-two thousand men to fight with him against the Midianites. But God told him, "The troops with you are too many for me to give the Midianites into their hand. Israel would only take the credit away from me, saying, 'My own hand has delivered me.'" So God pared them back to a mere three hundred men, less than one percent of the original army! The reason Gideon succeeded was not because of who he was, but because the Lord was with him.

If you feel that you do not have the right credentials to do what God has asked of you, you are probably right. But if God has called your name, he will be with you. He may even send an angel to give you a vision for who you really are: a mighty warrior determined to do God's will, take great risks, and make the necessary sacrifices in his service.

Lord, you know how weak I really am. I ask you to make my weakness raw material for your grace. Your power is made perfect in weakness such as mine. Thank you that you choose the foolish things of this world to confound the wise. Do great things in me, and then take your glory, Lord.

A Dream of Angels

*Mary had been engaged to Joseph, but before they lived to-
gether, she was found to be with child from the Holy Spirit.
Her husband Joseph, being a righteous man and unwilling to
expose her to public disgrace, planned to dismiss her quietly.
But just when he had resolved to do this, an angel of the Lord
appeared to him in a dream.*

—MATTHEW 1:18–20 NRSV

The angels played a major role in all the events surrounding
Jesus' birth, not the least of which was their role as messengers to Joseph. Three times this man saw angels in his dreams.
Once to convince him that the impossible had happened: Mary
was pregnant though she had not been unfaithful to him. Once to
warn him to take his family and flee to Egypt, where they would
be safe from Herod's wrath. And once to return to Israel after
Herod had died.

We don't know a great deal about Joseph, but we do know
that he must have been a man willing to take the risks that faith
required. As a young man Joseph must have had dreams for himself. His engagement to Mary may have marked the beginning of
a way of life he intended to live: to work hard, prosper, and raise
a family in Nazareth, as his father before him had done. But his
plans were disrupted by angels. He would flee Bethlehem with
Mary and the infant in the middle of the night, escaping to a for-

eign land to elude the wrath of a power-mad king. It would be many years before he would see Nazareth again.

Of course Joseph had a choice in the matter each time the angels appeared to him. The first time he could have brushed the angel off as nothing more than a product of his own wishful thinking. When in the long history of the world had a woman ever become pregnant without sleeping with a man? He could have set Mary aside as he had planned to do and married someone else. But Joseph heeded the angel and said yes to God's plan for his life.

Did Joseph comprehend the enormity of the decision he was making? Possibly, he did. But certainly, he could not foresee the strange mixture of blessing and suffering that lay in store for him and his family. His yes would cost him many sleepless nights, but it would also involve him in the greatest miracle of all time.

God has a dream for each one of us, and, sometimes that dream, interrupts the dream we have for our own lives. Like Joseph, we have a choice to make. We can reject the dream and move on with our life as planned. Or we can welcome the dream, even though we don't understand all the implications. If we say yes to God, we will encounter an adventure which will involve both agony and joy. In the end, it will have been well worth the risk. Ultimately, the choice is always ours.

My Father, help me to let go of lesser dreams, that I might fully grasp hold of every good thing you have for me. Let there not come a time when I let my yes become a maybe and my maybe become a no. Give me the courage to follow wherever you lead. Help me to dream the dreams you have for me.

*B*IBLIOGRAPHY ❧

Adler, Mortimer. *The Angels and Us* (New York: Macmillan, 1982)

Anderson, Joan Wester. *Where Angels Walk* (New York: Ballantine, 1992)

Bragg, Rick. "Tried by Deadly Tornado, an Anchor of Faith Holds," *New York Times,* April 3, 1994, p.1

Freedman, David Noel (ed.). *Anchor Bible Dictionary* (New York: Doubleday, 1992)

Graham, Billy. *Angels: God's Secret Agents* (Waco, TX: Word, 1986)

Henry, Matthew. *Matthew Henry's Commentary on the Whole Bible, Vol. I* (McLean, VA: MacDonal)

Herring, Wayne C. "Angelology," unpublished sermon.

Kinnaman, Gary. *Angels Dark and Light* (Ann Arbor, MI: Servant, 1994)

MacGregor, Geddes. *Angels* (New York: Paragon, 1988)

McKenzie, John L. *Dictionary of the Bible* (New York: Macmillan, 1965)

The Interpreter's Dictionary of the Bible (Nashville, TN: Abingdon, 1962)

O'Sullivan, Paul. *All About Angels* (Rockford, IL: Tan, 1945)

Ronner, John. *Do You Have a Guardian Angel?* (Murfreesboro, TN: Mamre, 1985)

Ronner, John. *Know Your Angels* (Murfreesboro, TN: Mamre, 1993)

Unger, Merrill F. *Unger's Bible Dictionary* (Chicago: Moody, 1957, 1961, 1966)